Integrating Blockchain into Supply Chain Management

Integrating Blockchain into Supply Chain Management

A toolkit for practical implementation

Remko Van Hoek
Brian Fugate
Marat Davletshin
Matthew A Waller

KoganPage

First published in Great Britain and the United States in 2020 by Kogan Page Limited

2nd Floor, 45 Gee Street	122 W 27th St, 10th Floor	4737/23 Ansari Road
London	New York, NY 10001	Daryaganj
EC1V 3RS	USA	New Delhi 110002
United Kingdom		India

www.koganpage.com

© Remko Van Hoek 2020

The right of Remko Van Hoek, Brian Fugate, Marat Davletshin and Matthew A Waller to be identified as the author of this work has been asserted by them in accordance with the Copyright, Designs and Patents Act 1988.

Hardback	978 1 78966 048 7
Paperback	978 0 74949 826 9
Ebook	978 0 74949 825 2

British Library Cataloguing-in-Publication Data

A CIP record for this book is available from the British Library.

Library of Congress Cataloging-in-Publication Data

Names: Hoek, Remko I. van, author.
Title: Integrating blockchain into supply chain management : a toolkit for practical implementation / Remko van Hoek [and three others].
Description: London ; New York : Kogan Page, 2020.
Identifiers: LCCN 2019013419 (print) | LCCN 2019014300 (ebook) | ISBN 9780749498252 (ebook) | ISBN 9781789660487 (hardback) | ISBN 9780749498269 (pbk.)
Subjects: LCSH: Business logistics–Technological innovations. | Blockchains (Databases)
Classification: LCC HD38.5 (ebook) | LCC HD38.5 .H627 2020 (print) | DDC 658.70285/57–dc23
LC record available at https://lccn.loc.gov/2019013419

Typeset by Hong Kong FIVE Workshop
Print production managed by Jellyfish
Printed and bound in Great Britain by CPI Group (UK) Ltd, Croydon CR0 4YY

To Susanne, Sophia, Grant, Luke, and Sarah

– Matt

To Jenny, Ally, Luke, Brynley, and Hudson

– Brian

To my family.
Maryl (for being my most patient coach and an image of
Mary the mother), Ticho (for being a great older brother),
Dylan (for being a great younger brother) and
Jason (for making our family complete), for Anja and Henk,
Cathy and Bob (for always being proud)

– Remko

CONTENTS

You can download resources for this book at
koganpage.com/IBSCM

ABOUT THE AUTHORS

Matthew A Waller is the dean of the Sam M Walton College of Business at the University of Arkansas, where he also serves as the Sam M Walton Leadership Chair and a professor of supply chain management. Matt joined the UA as a visiting assistant professor in 1994 and has held several positions over more than 20 years with the College of Business. He was the director of the executive MBA-China programme for two years, and the chair of the Department of Supply Chain Management when it was established in 2011. He also is an SEC Academic Leadership Fellow.

In addition to his work in academia, Matt was co-founder of, and a partner with, Bentonville Associates Ventures and co-founder and chief strategy officer for Mercari Technologies. A native of Kansas City, MO, he graduated summa cum laude with a bachelor's degree in economics from the University of Missouri. Then he earned a Master's degree in management science and a PhD in business logistics, both from Pennsylvania State University. Matt is co-author of *The Definitive Guide to Inventory Management* (Pearson Education, 2014). He also is the former co-editor of the *Journal of Business Logistics*, the leading academic journal in the discipline. And his opinion pieces have appeared in *The Wall Street Journal Asia* and *Financial Times*.

Brian Fugate is the Oren Harris Chair in Transportation, Chair of the Department of Supply Chain Management at the University of Arkansas, and MIT Fulbright Senior Research Scholar. He teaches supply chain management courses and is the co-editor-in-chief of the *Journal of Supply Chain Management*. His research focuses on advancing the scholarship and practice of strategic, global integration of demand and supply, knowledge flows, and sustainability across the supply chain.

Brian's diverse background in business and academia began on his parents' cattle and pig farm in eastern Tennessee, where he developed an interest in agriculture and learned the value of hard work. He earned a degree in industrial engineering at the University of Tennessee, then worked in the airline and auto industries before returning to UT for an MBA in logistics and marketing and, later, a PhD. Brian was a professor at Lehigh University and Colorado State University before joining the staff at the University of Arkansas. While in Colorado, Brian and a partner developed ACTIV82LRN, an online application that allows students to engage in social learning by answering questions while viewing and evaluating the answers of fellow students. The app earned an Innovations That Inspire award from the Association to Advance Collegiate Schools of Business (AACSB).

His work has been featured in many publications, including the *Journal of Supply Chain Management*, *Journal of Business Logistics* and *Journal of Operations Management*.

Remko Van Hoek, a professor of supply chain management in the Walton College of Business at the University of Arkansas, has extensive experience in the corporate and academic worlds. The former chief procurement officer for the Walt Disney Company has held senior supply chain executive roles in the United States and Europe at several companies, including Nike and PwC. And he previously taught as a professor and/or visiting professor at Cranfield School of Management in England, Rotterdam School of Management in the Netherlands and Vlerick School of Management in Belgium.

Remko has served for more than 10 years on the board of directors for the Council of Supply Chain Management Professionals (CSCMP), the leading professional and academic association in supply chain management, including as the 2017–18 Board Chair. He serves on four editorial advisory boards, was European editor of *International Journal of Physical Distribution and Logistics Management* (IJPDLM) and has more than 70 publications in international peer-reviewed journals, including *Journal of Operations Management*, *Journal of Business Logistics* and *Harvard Business Review*. He also holds a fellowship from the Chartered Institute of Logistics and Transport (CILT) and the Chartered Institute of Procurement and Supply (CIPS).

Remko, who earned a PhD in international economics from Utrecht University in the Netherlands, is co-author of *Logistics*

Management and Strategy (Pearson Education, 2014, 5th edition) and *Leading Procurement Strategy* (Kogan Page, 2018, 2nd edition, two language translations). He is the only person on the top 10 list of thought leaders in supply chain, the top 10 textbooks in supply chain and the top 10 books for executives in supply chain.

Marat Davletshin is a third-year PhD student in the Walton College of Business at the University of Arkansas. He grew up in Russia and moved to the United States in 2010 to attend the Simon Business School at the University of Rochester in New York. After earning an MBA, Marat spent nearly three years as an operations manager with Amazon, then returned to academia at the University of Arkansas. He is pursuing a doctorate in supply chain management with a goal of a long-term career in academic research on issues related to supply networks and operations management. Marat's doctoral work focuses on applying network theories used in physics to supply networks and emerging technologies.

FOREWORD

Blockchain. For now, it is almost as mysterious as the universe itself. Fortunately, these terrific supply chain aficionados took it upon themselves to research and write a book that both helps us understand blockchain and provides a process for deciding whether it makes sense to use it.

I have had the pleasure of knowing three of the authors – Matt Waller, Brian Fugate, and Remko Van Hoek – for a couple of decades now. It's no surprise to me that these inquisitive experts from the Walton College of Business decided to tackle this project. The Walton College for years has produced excellent supply chain thought, research, and practical knowledge. And as president and CEO of the Council of Supply Chain Management Professionals, I've witnessed first hand how the authors have shaped, and continue to shape, our discipline with their wide array of experiences. They help ensure that we – CSCMP and the entire supply chain management field – innovate, evolve, and remain relevant, which in many ways is the heartbeat of our industry.

Supply chain management is very much like the switch and the light. We flip the switch and the light comes on, but we don't call our power company and thank them. We don't spend time thinking about how the light came on. We give it very little thought, unless, of course, we flip the switch and nothing happens. And when do supply chain folks get called? When something goes wrong.

But that's changing, and in many ways has changed, largely because innovations in technology (such as blockchain) have helped supply chain professionals become more valued voices within their organizations and industries. We have seen our field grow from a cost to be managed to a powerful weapon in modern global business. Back in 1980, logistics costs in the United States were about 16 percent of GDP; today, they are 7.7 percent (or about $1.5 trillion). We have gotten more productive, more efficient, and more sophisticated with our technologies, allowing for the redeployment of people to more value-added positions.

I know I am biased about our discipline and its impact, but I'm confident supply chain management improves the financial position of companies and economies. Our stature and credibility are increasing, and innovations with technology are a huge reason. We have benefited from decades of technologies and subsequent systems, with improved business processes built on top. Those processes have been successful because innovative and creative leaders took risks, experimented, and used technology to develop new and better ways of working. New technology without changes in the way we do business only leaves us with more expensive technology. Modern supply chain leaders are perfectly positioned to prove (or disprove) that the technology is, in fact, worthy of implementing.

That will happen with blockchain, and this book will help make it happen.

Blockchain, as the authors note, is of high interest to leaders, yet with less understanding and even less activity at the moment. That undoubtedly will change if, as many suspect, this technology becomes a foundation for a better process that supply chain leaders can employ. For now, a variety of pioneers and early adopters are paving the way. The authors interviewed many of these individuals, from different industries and with a variety of understanding of blockchain, to provide a foundation of where we are, where we're going, and how to best get there. Understandably, some of these practitioners remain sceptical, but others shifted their views substantially once they knew more. Several have bought into the idea that blockchain can introduce a change that creates, as Harvard professors Marco Iansiti and Karim Lakhani put it, "new foundations for our economic and social systems". All agree only time will tell and there's much to learn, experience, and prove.

New technologies take time to implement, and they typically result in a better process than what existed before. Once installed and put into use, they become almost commonplace and we wonder how we accomplished these things in the past. Paul Lothian, a business solutions architect for Tyson Foods put it this way when interviewed by the authors: "I believe it [blockchain] will be important, but the average Joe doesn't need to know it's affecting him until it's already affecting him."

This book is for leaders, especially leaders in supply chain management, who want to be ahead of that knowledge curve. They want to understand blockchain's potential for the supply chain and, if it makes sense, use it to keep pace (or move ahead of) their competition. They don't want to be caught off guard or left behind by the places this technology takes us.

If you go back in time, many of the technologies that are inherent in modern supply chains went through the same exploratory process. I recall the early days of RFID. There were sceptics, early adopters, and those who really thought it would have major positive implications. What was then seemingly impossible is now a very functional part of our global supply chain experience. We are in a similar time with blockchain.

It is critical that the early stages of what can be a foundational change in supply chain management is supported by the diligence the authors have demonstrated. This book describes how blockchain applies and can apply to supply chain management. The notion of a "transparent" supply chain, where information is available to all key participants at the same time and cannot be altered, is very logical. The authors provide insight into why it's so difficult, and what could be done about it.

They also provide a real road map to get going. This is often the most difficult step in any journey. They take us through definitions, and there are several, and into use cases and pilots. Importantly, they also explain how to evaluate pilots and provide insight into dealing with the plethora of opinions of value that will likely emerge.

No one has all the answers. But the authors' research and deep passion to find out all we can and anticipate future options is laid out in an easy-to-understand fashion. The most successful supply chain leaders by their very nature are inquisitive about new technologies. They'll absorb this content and make their own judgments, but they will certainly be better equipped as the blockchain future unfolds.

I had the pleasure of spending twenty-five years in the food industry, learning and leading supply chains and the organizations that made great strides by using new technologies. I vividly recall the leaders who took it upon themselves to research and advance difficult concepts, most of which became realities that we all benefit from today. This is what is happening with our authors and this book regarding blockchain. I love and I am passionate about this discipline. This book matters, and I know you will not only enjoy it, but that by reading it you will be so much better prepared for the journey.

Rick Blasgen
President and CEO, Council of
Supply Chain Management Professionals (CSCMP)

PREFACE

The Walton College of Business at the University of Arkansas has quickly become a leading institution in understanding blockchain and the evaluation of practical business uses for the technology.

Interestingly, or some might say oddly, at least some credit for that reality and, as a by-product, for this book itself goes to a couple of Canadian economics professors, Leonard Dudley and Pierre Lasserre. In January 1989, the *European Economic Review* published an esoteric article by Dudley and Lasserre titled "Information as a Substitute for Inventories" which found its way into the hands of an aspiring graduate student: me. The article has affected the remainder of my career, so its influence is felt throughout the Walton College, where I've been dean since 2015. And it is at the root of my interest in and appreciation for blockchain technology.

To explain this connection simply, I can start with one paragraph from the abstract of Dudley and Lasserre's article:

> The ratio of inventories to sales in North American manufacturing has fallen without the offsetting increases in unfilled orders or price variation that are predicted by some theoretical models… in the face of falling relative costs of communications, firms will substitute information for inventories, thereby allowing their production systems to absorb a greater part of demand shocks.

Firms carry safety stock extra inventory because they are uncertain about demand and lead time. If communication is less expensive, more timely, more accurate, etc, then sometimes we can learn about increases in demand early enough to address them with extra production or larger purchases, thereby avoiding out-of-stocks. Or we might learn that an order will arrive later than expected, rather than being surprised by a late delivery. The power of information in these situations makes perfect sense today. But this article was written prior to the advent of the World Wide Web, and most people at that time knew nothing about the internet or email. That's what made the article so cutting-edge and influential.

Most of my research over the next two and a half decades had to do with inventory management and forecasting and the use of information to improve both of these tasks. I even wrote a book on the topic. Some of my research looked at new ways of collaboration between suppliers and buyers to allow for information to substitute for inventory. Some of it looked at new ways of using point of sale data, order data, and shipment data to improve forecasts, thus reducing the need for inventory. I also researched how different types of inventory management systems could use information more effectively to reduce inventory and improve forecasts.

This wasn't just an academic passion. I also founded a consulting firm that specialized in helping businesses use my research findings, as well as a complementary software company. I even have a patent that addresses this issue in the context of retail shelf inventory and layout.

As my career progressed, it became clear that information also substitutes for transportation costs, warehousing costs, material handling costs, and many other costs. In fact, information can make total supply chain costs lower and make supply chains more effective and resilient.

When blockchain began emerging a few years ago as a technology related to cryptocurrency, it seemed logical that it could have an impact on the flow of information as well as currency. I started listening to podcasts and reading everything I could find about it. It quickly struck me that blockchain could possibly revolutionize data visibility, make information immutable, and improve collaboration and trust. As a result, it could possibly have a more significant impact on supply chain efficiency than the World Wide Web.

While I found myself driven to learn all I could about blockchain, the technology also soon became an important pursuit of the Sam M Walton College of Business. As the dean, I have a responsibility to ensure that we focus on things that fit our vision and mission. And since the vision of the Walton College is to be a thought leader and a catalyst for transforming lives, I was easily sold by faculty who wanted to push us to the leading edge when it came to researching and teaching about blockchain and its applications. Our Blockchain Center of Excellence, for instance, focuses specifically on discovering and sharing innovative uses of blockchain. Its director, Mary Lacity, used her pioneering research as the foundation for one of the first business-focused books on the technology, *A Manager's Guide to Blockchain for Business*, and she and her book provided invaluable insights for this book.

Our Information Systems Department, meanwhile, has led an interdisciplinary approach to studying blockchain's potential impact on business in general and on specific disciplines, including supply chain management. The IS Department was teaching blockchain in multiple classes in 2017, which is also when it held its first "blockchain hackathon" which allowed students to work on real blockchain solutions with interested business partners. The Walton College also held two major conferences for business leaders on blockchain in 2018, and that fall we offered a cryptocurrency class through our Department of Finance, as well as another blockchain hackathon.

This book, which provides a researched guide for how blockchain applies (and will apply) to supply chain management, fits perfectly within the mission of the college, as well as the interests and expertise of its co-authors. Sharing the content allows us to move toward thought leadership in the area of supply chain management and blockchain technology. The research required to create this book pushed us to new limits, and we believe the lessons we learned and that we will share in these pages can serve as a catalyst for transforming lives, not only for the supply chain professionals who will put what we've learned to use in their businesses but for everyone who will benefit from a smarter supply chain.

The genesis of this book began when two of the co-authors, Brian Fugate and Marat Davletshin, witnessed an emerging trend and a parallel emerging need. The trend, of course, was the growing interest in blockchain's potential applications throughout the supply chain, and the need was the desire among business leaders to wisely sort through the hype and make responsible decisions about if, when, and how to explore the uses of blockchain. Brian, the chair of our supply chain department, and Marat, a graduate student with an expertise in network theory, shared some of their ideas and early research with me, and we quickly agreed to pursue the book. A few months later Remko Van Hoek joined our faculty, and his background and interests made him a logical partner who could elevate the work we were doing.

In roughly two years of focused research, we read countless books and articles, watched videos, listened to podcasts, attended conferences, put on conferences, conducted our own research survey, and interviewed around two dozen leaders from companies and organizations that are pioneering the use of blockchain in the supply chain from a rural farming cooperative like Grass Roots to international standards organization like GS1, from global retailers like Walmart to logistics giants like Maersk.

Fortunately, my co-authors and I live in Northwest Arkansas, where there is a flurry of activity and interest in blockchain applications. Walmart, J.B. Hunt Transport, Tyson Foods, ArcBest... even our governor. They've all been early investigators, and in some cases pioneers, of developing practical, business applications for blockchain.

All of this made it easy for us to connect to key leaders who are advancing blockchain technology in the supply chain. But we were also able to bring in leading voices from around the world as we explored not only what the technology can do in and for the supply chain, but how practitioners can go about developing and testing uses cases as they seek to improve their business efficiencies. What they'll find in blockchain is a powerful tool that can enrich and empower their use of information. And if they use that information effectively, it very well could transform the supply chains they manage for decades to come.

Matt Waller
Dean, Sam M Walton College of Business
University of Arkansas

References

Dudley, L and Lasserre P (1989) Information as a substitute for inventories, *European Economic Review* 1 (**33**), pages 67–88 (January)

USING THIS BOOK

Developments in information technology are rapidly changing the supply chain management rulebook. Thanks to the World Wide Web, we now have access to unprecedented amounts of data and computing power, providing the foundation needed for the development of artificial intelligence (AI), the Internet of Things (IoT) and blockchain applications that will allow us to automate as opposed to digitize supply chain operations. Of these technologies, blockchain is not only the newest, but probably conceptually and practically the most difficult to comprehend. And while there have been ample academic, trade and popular publications on blockchain, these publications are either too technical or lack the necessary depth to be of use to supply chain management practitioners and researchers.

Integrating Blockchain into Supply Chain Management demystifies the use of blockchain in the supply chain, providing the reader with insight and awareness of blockchain technology and how to integrate it into a business plan as an effective supply chain tool.

The content of the book has been structured as follows:

- Chapters 1 and 2 provide a contextual understanding of supply chain management. Beginning with a historical perspective, we look at the specific challenges of today's supply chain as well as introducing a number of concepts and the SCOR model that are used later on in the book.

- Chapters 3 and 4 provide an introduction to blockchain, AI, and IoT, giving the reader the required technology background for the rest of the book. Complex concepts such as hashing algorithms and asymmetric cryptography are explained in an intuitive way.

- Chapters 5 and 6 are bridging chapters, integrating the supply chain management chapters with the technology chapters. Hence, these chapters focus on the discussion of the problems in the supply chain for which blockchain is an actual solution and what the expected impact is in terms of supply chain performance of the technology.

- Chapters 7 and 8 feature actual blockchain use cases, offering an in-depth look at the opportunities and challenges that blockchain and the other technologies have to offer. The last chapter of the book addresses the business case for innovation.

As each of the chapters can be read in isolation, instructors are free to mix and match the chapters, based on their specific needs. However, we do advise keeping the structure of the book in mind. Supplementary to the book, various online resources have been created to further enhance your learning in this subject matter. These online resources include slides, discussion questions, case study research ideas and so on and will be made available on the Kogan Page website.

ACKNOWLEDGEMENTS

Writing a book that involves blockchain is like chasing a piece of paper that's caught in a tornado – you can't match its speed or predict its course, so you keep pace as best you can and hope it lands somewhere in your general vicinity. We began this project realizing that blockchain is a moving target, but also realizing that there are some bedrock truths involved with the technology and with supply chain management that allow us to connect the two in ways that stand the tests of time.

Doing that, however required a great deal of help and input from countless sources. We read books, articles, academic papers and the like. We listened to podcasts and video interviews. We attended conferences, some of which included us on their platforms. And, of course, we talked to people. Lots and lots of people.

In some cases, relevant parts of those discussions are shared in the book. In others, the value was primarily in the details, insights and direction the experts provided. Regardless, we are thankful to all who gave us their time and their wisdom, including: Paul Chang, IBM; Cameron Geiger, Walmart; Dennis Gerson, IBM; Michael Gibbs, Walton College of Business; Erik Hansen, Kansas City Southern Railway; Cody Hopkins, Grass Roots; Jeffrey Keller, IBM; Mary Lacity, Blockchain Center of Excellence, Walton College of Business, University of Arkansas; Paul Lothian, Tyson Foods; John Monarch, ShipChain; Gena Morgan, GS1 US; Mike Naatz, Kansas City Southern Railway; Ranjit Notani, One Network; Melanie Nuce, GS1 US; Dan Sanker, CaseStack; Zach Steelman, Walton College of Business; Michael White, TradeLens/Maersk; Bill Wilson, Coca-Cola; Frank Yiannas, the FDA (formerly Walmart); Kevin Yoder, ArcBest. There were also a few sources for this project who provided insights and examples but needed us to withhold their names and company names. We're thankful to them, as well.

We're also thankful to the administration and staff at the University of Arkansas, who not only allowed us to work on this project but encoraged and supported it. Casey Spatz, the administrative support supervisor for the supply chain management department, was particularly helpful in getting interviews transcribed.

We also are indebted to Stephen Caldwell for his help with the writing, to Julia Swales at Kogan Page for believing in this book and for helping us navigate the challenges of getting it published, and to Kogan Page's Ro'isin Singh for her exceptional developmental edits.

Pain of the chain

We recognized the look on the manager's face: uncertainty... confusion... anxiety... helplessness... put them all in a bucket, shake them up, and you'll get some form of what we were seeing. If you had stumbled into the meeting, you might have thought we had asked him to explain the impossible – like how *déjà vu* works or how to understand the emotions of a typical teenager. It was even worse: we had asked about... blockchain.

The advent of new technologies – most notably blockchain – has the potential to radically transform how transactions are recorded, stored and used throughout supply networks. The result: a transparent supply chain that, if the hype holds true, will usher in unprecedented levels of visibility, accountability, efficiencies, collaboration and trust.

Bringing this revolution to life in a way that benefits companies and consumers alike, however, will likely take years of trial and error. It's the "error" part that has many supply chain managers and decision-makers nervous. In the high-speed competitive landscape of modern business, errors – even errors made in the name of progress – cost time and money, and that can cost a business... well... its business.

Smart leaders don't take risks without understanding the challenges and the potential rewards, and that's what makes any significant technology innovation so disruptively difficult. Supply chain veterans have lived through the challenges of aligning on standards for technologies like electronic data interchange (EDI) or the slower-than-predicted adoption of technologies like radio-frequency identification (RFID). At the same time, they recognize the potential benefits that new technologies might bring to their operations. So, when we talk to supply chain practitioners about blockchain, it's not surprising that they typically respond with something like this: "I don't really understand it. I don't really know what to do with it. I don't know exactly how it applies to our business, if it applies to our business, or if it ever will apply to our business. I just know that I need to figure it out. But I have no clue how to begin."

Kevin Yoder, Associate Director of Innovation Financial Management at ArcBest Technologies, is among the thousands of business leaders who are trying to "figure it out". Yoder was a panellist during one of the blockchain conferences hosted by the Walton College of Business at the University of Arkansas in 2018, and he pointed out at the time that he and his team were working furiously to understand blockchain's impact on their business. "We are being bombarded by interest in this from across the organization," he told the 230 attendees.

Like other leaders, Yoder wants to develop an appropriate strategy that makes sense for his business. And while the strategy, not technology, needs to drive the business decisions, he knows you can't develop a sound strategy around blockchain without understanding the technology and how it applies in practical, beneficial ways to real supply chain problems.

We have analysed and synthesized countless hours of interviews and mounds of research to sort through the hype of blockchain and provide some clarity around what it really means to the future of supply chain management – and, more specifically, to supply chain professionals. And we very quickly realized that what most of them need is a toolkit that helps them understand the potential of blockchain for their business, the risks involved, and the processes for developing and implementing use cases that could lead to potentially valuable new systems and processes.

This conclusion is supported by several surveys, including our own benchmarking study. We surveyed procurement and supply chain professionals around the world, from Finland to Singapore, from the Netherlands to the United States, to evaluate the state of play of blockchain in the supply chain and to map a path towards potential adoption and implementation. The findings were both interesting and enlightening.

The bars in Figure 1.1 show the average scores for eight bench-mark questions we asked. The scale ranges from 1 ("not at all") to 3 ("partially so") to 5 ("very much so").

The first three bars paint a picture of interest. Operational management and executives are interested in and engaged in learning about blockchain, because, as bar one indicates, they recognize the potential that the technology holds for the supply chain.

The final three bars, however, paint a picture of uncertainty. The survey indicates leaders are not really sure how to get started and how to tackle the opportunity. In other words, leaders are interested and engaged but many don't have a strategy, a roadmap, or resources allocated towards creating a solution. That's what makes this book so relevant, because it helps answers key questions like *How are we going to get going?* And *How are we going to respond when asked what we are doing with blockchain in our supply chain?*

The middle two bars, paradoxically, paint a picture of activity. Companies are piloting blockchain in their supply chains and creating business cases for using it. We can learn from these companies and, as mentioned, we included several of them in our research for this book. They provide insights on if you should attempt a pilot, on the ins and outs of how to get started, and on what to look for during and after that process. On the other hand, as Walmart executive Cameron Geiger pointed out, there's an obvious cause for concern in the horseshoe-shaped curve seen in these results.

"What worries me is the gap between executive excitement and business strategy," Geiger, a senior vice president at Walmart responsible for supply chain technology product, told us when we reviewed the results in his Bentonville, AR, office. "We see that many in the industry are beginning to pilot before they have a strategy or a team. So where are they going and who is taking them there? Is this a solution looking for a problem?" (Geiger, 2018).

MHI, an association representing material handling, logistics and supply chain professionals, found similar results when it partnered with Deloitte to survey more than one thousand executives for its 2018 Annual Industry Report (2018). Only 6 per cent of the executives reported blockchain was "in use" within their organization, but 53 per cent predicted it would be in use within five years and 70 per cent said blockchain would either "support ongoing improvements"

Figure 1.1 Blockchain state of play

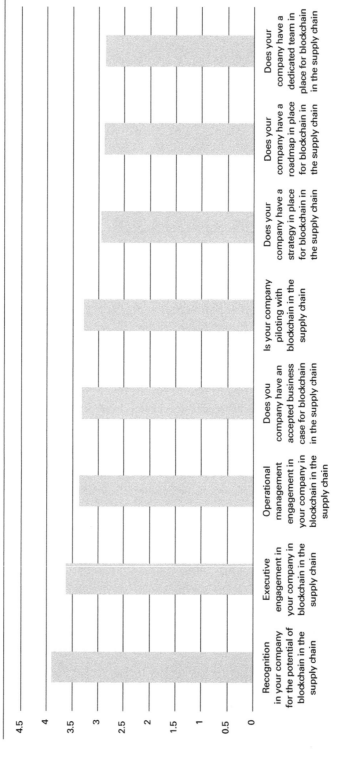

in their organization or had the potential to "disrupt or create competitive advantage". Of the 11 emerging technologies the study considered, only artificial intelligence had an adoption rate as low as blockchain.

What we're seeing, in other words, is a curve that shows high interest in blockchain among executives, less understanding, and even less activity when it comes to creating business cases and implementing solutions. Executives and managers recognize that blockchain holds potential and there is lots of interest in trying out blockchain, but most companies need help developing pilots, business cases and getting teams in place to actually develop and conduct the pilots. This comes as no surprise, because the technology is emerging and everyone involved, from the programmers to the executives, are still exploring its benefits and limits. As MHI CEO George Prest told *Supply Chain Dive*, "Everybody is still trying to really figure out what blockchain is all about" (Branch and Lopez, 2018).

These findings were confirmed and illuminated later in 2018 when we held an interactive workshop on blockchain in the supply chain for alumni of the Walton College of Business executive MBA programme. Prior to the workshop, the 58 participants completed a survey, and we used the results as discussion points during the session. While the group was small from a statistical perspective, it was significant in its composition – the participants ranged from managers to vice presidents and represented a variety of industries, including retail (14), consumer products companies (12), professional and financial services (12), and logistics services (4).

Only 22 per cent of these respondents said their companies were either developing use cases or pilots, or implementing a blockchain solution in their supply chain. And 39 per cent of the participating companies were not yet formally considering blockchain in the supply chain (see Figure 1.2).

The participants at this event echoed our other findings – that while leaders are interested in and to a great extent exploring options with blockchain, they continue to wrestle with questions about things such as how it might scale and what type of return on investment they can expect (questions we will explore in great depth throughout this book).

Figure 1.2   Degree of adoption

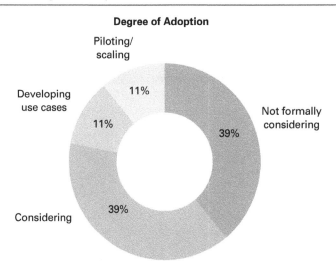

For now, a handful of larger companies like IBM, Microsoft, Walmart, Maersk, Unilever, FedEx and Kansas City Southern are paving the way when it comes to implementing blockchain. Dennis Gerson, an engineer and technical adviser at IBM, estimated that 75 per cent of Fortune 400 companies had tested blockchain as of late 2018 – not just played around in a technology sandbox, but had actually "tested a hypothesis and were seeing what happens". But, he added, 90 per cent of those never make it past the pilot.

The successful pilots, however, are not creating transformative change – at least not yet – and for supply chain managers, that's what this is really all about, isn't it? Creating process improvements that actually result in significantly better overall supply chains. That's not happening, at least not yet. But there's a clear path for making it happen using blockchain.

Consider the potential value of blockchain for supply chain networks when it's represented in a simple two-by-two chart (Figure 1.3) that shows how human interactions might work with technology to create transformative change.

Most companies that are experimenting with blockchain are seeing results in the bottom left quadrant – they are gaining visibility into existing processes and access to information they can use. For example, one of the best-known test cases for blockchain involved

Figure 1.3   Value of blockchain for supply networks

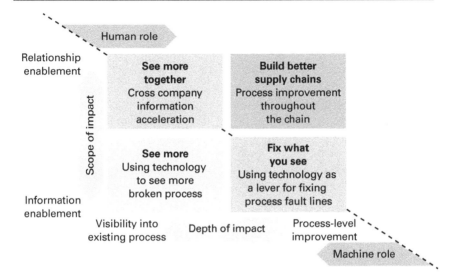

tracking mangoes from farms in Mexico to Walmart's stores in the United States. The initial test involved only a few key players in the supply chain and primarily offered faster visibility into the process (bottom left). The time it took to trace a mango back to the farm of origin went from six days, 18 hours and 26 minutes down to 2.2 seconds. It didn't fundamentally change anything about the supply chain processes that were used, but it allowed Walmart to gain access to important information much more quickly than it could before.

"Most of the use cases and pilots that we see are stuck in the bottom left," Geiger told us. "These pilots simply bring a new technology to an old problem without really solving it. For instance, if you have bad data quality, you are just going to move your bad data faster"(Geiger, 2018).

When multiple players who are involved in the supply network all have access to the information on the blockchain, however, you then move to the upper left quadrant. Internally, everyone from buyers to store managers might have an interest in seeing the information collected on the mango blockchain. Externally, that information would be valuable to farmers, the processing plants, the transportation companies, and agencies within governments.

The launch version of the famous Maersk and IBM blockchain partnership falls in this quadrant. TradeLens, the blockchain platform created by the two companies, launched an early adopter programme in August 2018 and expected to have a fully working version by the start of 2019. Even in early adopter mode, the platform had more than a hundred participants providing global shipping data and literally hundreds of millions of "shipping events" for all the partners to see and use. So, they are sharing more shipping documents and information across the supply chain faster and earlier. This does not mean they have changed anything about what they do with this information, but they are enabling across relationships the ability to "see more together".

Piloting blockchain almost always provides greater visibility – it puts you in the two boxes on the left. The question then becomes, what do you do with it? Can the technology actually be used to improve processes? Can you work with partners to develop systemic improvements throughout the chain? If you can't, then blockchain may still be worth using for the visibility benefits alone. But if you can, then blockchain becomes transformative.

In some cases, the visibility could lead to technology-based process improvements (bottom right). For instance, blockchain has the potential to eliminate time-consuming paperwork at ports and other border crossings, which could move the mangoes from farm to store more quickly, thus providing longer shelf life for the product. Michael White, the TradeLens leader for Maersk, told us the most basic fix for the global shipping industry by using their blockchain-enabled platform involves the ability to efficiently answer the simplest of questions: Where is my container? "Instead of having five different people check ten different companies to find out the status of boxes or a shipment," he told us, "they can do it with one person with one platform" (White, 2018).

ClearWay, the beta product released by TradeLens, focuses on digitizing documents in global shipping, which figures to create enormous efficiencies for importers, exporters, brokers, customs and other government agencies, and non-government organizations as they collaborate to ship goods. Ultimately, blockchain users want to move towards a better supply chain, which comes from those types of shared process improvements throughout the supply network. That's the holy grail represented by the upper right quadrant.

Note that as we move from the bottom left to the top right, the focus shifts beyond adopting blockchain as a new technology and moves towards leveraging a new technology in how we build and run supply chains. This requires human beings who provide analysis and insights and then act upon the technology's potential. The technology might expose bad data and broken processes, but it's not going to clean up data or fix broken processes. Humans need to do this. And that is why a toolkit, a collaborative team and the hands-on engagement of supply chain managers are key to reaching the upper right quadrant. There are no shortcuts to victory and the technology itself does not excuse us from needing to do the right thing – to build better supply chains.

We know of no instances where a company or industry using blockchain has truly reached the nirvana of the upper right quadrant. But such a transformation takes time, and several pioneers appear at least headed in the right direction. In the mango case, former Walmart Vice President of Food Safety Frank Yiannas points out that the value of blockchain is not what it did with the mangoes but what it can do with the complex food supply chain.

Shortly after announcing the results of the test case with mangoes, Yiannas said he was talking to the leader of a large dairy company about the pilot. "Why do we need blockchain to do that?" the leader asked Yiannas. "I can do that in our system" (Yiannas, 2017).

There are existing systems, Yiannas acknowledged, that could replicate the mango test case. But, he added, "You can't do that with 70,000 food SKUs that have different suppliers that don't all align with your system. Everybody isn't in your system and you don't have interfaces with everybody else's system. Blockchain is a game changer for being able to do all of these transactions" (Yiannas, 2017).

It's those "game-changer" types of promises that have supply chain leaders – in small companies as well as large – intrigued about blockchain. But, as our survey indicated, most of them are lacking a strategy or roadmap.

"As more people have an interest in this," Yiannas, now Deputy Commissioner for Food Policy and Response at the FDA, told us, "they're grappling with where do I begin and how to I think about it? So, documenting a playbook and case studies and stories is a great idea.... I'm looking for good books on blockchain. I want people to learn about it, and people ask me what they should be reading. There are not a lot of good books out there" (Yiannas, 2017).

Our goal with this book is to help decision-makers at all levels of supply chain management understand blockchain and, more importantly, evaluate the value proposition the technology brings, or doesn't bring, to their work. Then we will guide you through the essential processes for making informed, practical, timely and business-savvy decisions about how – or if – you can effectively incorporate blockchain into your systems and processes. In short, we will help you:

- understand blockchain as a technology;
- understand the power of hype and the path to adoption;
- understand if and how blockchain applies to your type of supply chain network;
- understand the potential impacts on the key segments of modern supply chain management;
- apply ground-breaking research on using network theory when implementing blockchain in supply chains;
- develop your use case (if there is one);
- develop your business case (if you have a legitimate use case);
- create and manage a pilot for your blockchain test;
- effectively measure the results of your pilot;
- decide what to do next based on what you learn from your pilot.

We'll walk through this discussion in three stages (Figure 1.4). Part I will explain blockchain and how it connects to supply chain management. Part II will explore how blockchain will affect key areas of supply ecosystems. And Part III will delve into the challenges of creating a use case and running and evaluating a pilot with blockchain.

By providing the information and tools you need, you can prepare for the inevitable challenges and opportunities on the horizon. For some businesses, blockchain is an immediate play – a technology they

Figure 1.4   The path of the book

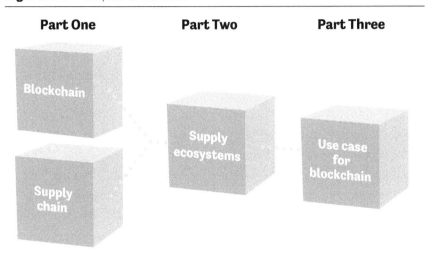

need to latch onto and implement as soon as possible. For a few, the technology won't filter down to their business operations for years, perhaps even decades. For most, however, the waves of transformation are beginning, and the time to prepare for all that's sure to come is now.

Yiannas once considered himself a blockchain sceptic, but now he's one of its biggest champions, not just as a way to improve food safety but as a tool that can add value throughout the supply chain process. He's quick to advise other leaders to start planning for the possibility of incorporating blockchain into their future business.

"My advice in general, especially if you're of any size, is to not wait too long," Yiannas told us. "Some of these technologies can emerge really quickly and you can get left behind really fast. I go back to the idea that this will allow people to be smarter and run a smarter supply chain. You don't want to be left behind and find that everyone competing with you is a lot smarter than you. That's a bad place to be" (Yiannas, 2017).

Fred Smith, the founder and CEO of FedEx and another blockchain proponent, expressed a similar warning during a panel discussion at Consensus 2018, a three-day conference on cryptocurrency and blockchain. "If you are not operating at the edge of new technologies," Smith said, "you will surely be disrupted. If you are not willing to embrace new technologies like Internet of Things and blockchain to face those new threats, you are, maybe subtly, at some point… going to extinction" (Zhao, 2018).

But even an ardent blockchain believer like Yiannas realizes the predicted revolution is in the early stages of a long journey to maturity. He believes pioneer investors (like Walmart) will lead to early adopters that eventually will lay the foundations for long-term, large-scale sustainable uses of blockchain among businesses. "It's the equivalent of building the interstate highway system," he said. "We're pouring cement. Once we pour all the cement, things will start to happen. Goods will start to flow and people will start to travel" (Yiannas, 2017).

Because this evolution will likely take years to mature into something widely accepted and used, some observers believe blockchain is a *foundational* technology as opposed to a *disruptive* technology. Marco Iansiti and Karim Lakhani, who are professors at Harvard Business School, have said it won't "attack a traditional business model with a lower-cost solution and overtake incumbent firms quickly". Instead, it potentially will "create new foundations for our economic and social systems. But while the impact will be enormous, it will take decades for blockchain to seep into our economic and social infrastructure. The process of adoption will be gradual and steady, not sudden, as waves of technological and institutional change gain momentum" (Iansiti and Lakhani, 2017).

For supply chain leaders, however, blockchain *feels* disruptive because of the enormous hype. It seems very much like a storm they know is coming, but they aren't sure whether to batten down the hatches, abandon ship or hang ten on the coming waves. They hear about it from colleagues, in industry blogs and in the popular press. And they rightly worry that failing to prepare for blockchain is the same thing as preparing them to fail. They want to know the value proposition blockchain brings, or doesn't bring, to their business so they can make informed, practical, timely and business-savvy decisions about how it applies to their work. But they need help sorting through the jargon-laced promises, understanding what this technology really does, and figuring out if, when and how they should adopt it.

The future of this transparent supply chain is, in many ways, yet to be defined. That's the nature of an evolving technology. But in researching blockchain and its potential uses across supply networks, we've come to one undeniable conclusion: business leaders need to sort through today's hype and prepare for a future that includes the technology – regardless of what it is today or what it morphs into over the coming years – or else, as Yiannas and Smith both warned, they'll soon find themselves scrambling to catch up with their competition.

Michael J Casey, a senior adviser for blockchain research at MIT's Digital Currency Initiative, put it this way: blockchain is "a technology of tomorrow, not today… (but) the future to which blockchains belong is coming so fast that a failure to properly strategize and to consider the widest range of design possibilities could eventually prove fatal for many businesses" (Casey, 2017).

Paul Lothian, for one, is keeping a watchful eye on the technology's progress. Lothian is a business solutions architect for Tyson Foods, Inc, which makes him what we'll call an "interested party" in the blockchain discussion. He has worked at Tyson since the late 1970s, and, as he put it, he's been involved with most of the company's "operational and distribution systems at one point or another" while learning the ins and outs of its ever-evolving role in the global food industry.

Over the years, Lothian has become deeply involved in issues like standards, traceability, logistics and supplier–vendor relationships. He's served on a variety of committees for GS1, the non-profit that establishes global product standards like labelling systems and universal barcodes. And he was part of a multidisciplinary group formed by the Institute for Food Technologists, which works on solving food safety issues. So, Lothian vigilantly tracks developments in blockchain and the technology's potential impact on Tyson, its business partners and the supply chain industry. "Most of the people I'm around who bring up blockchain have no clue how it works, but they've heard about it," he told us. "The question becomes, 'Do I need to know more about it?'" (Lothian, 2017).

And how does he answer that question? "I believe it will be important," he said, "but the average Joe doesn't need to know it's affecting him until it's already affecting him. I remember attending a conference back in 1984, and a guy from the university was there talking about this new network they had that was allowing them to share all this information among all the academic institutions. They were using TCP/IP. Did that become a big deal? Yeah. That's the internet. But did I have to learn anything about the internet? No, it just evolved. There will have to be players initially who understand the technologies around blockchain, but things will get developed and it will evolve" (Lothian, 2017).

While Lothian has little interest in learning the ins and outs of the programming, he has developed a basic understanding of what blockchain technology does and how it works. And that's the approach we're seeing from more and more supply chain professionals. Some organizations, including Tyson, have created an in-house cross-functional committee tasked with investigating the potential of blockchain technology. Other supply chain professionals are doing research on their own. Most are taking a wait-and-see approach when it comes to actually investing company funds and resources into blockchain. But very few are ignoring it.

Wherever you are on that continuum, this book will help to you move forward with confidence.

Chain links: Key points from this chapter

- New technologies like blockchain have the potential to fully digitize transactions and records throughout supply networks. The result: a transparent supply chain that, if the hype holds true, will usher in unprecedented levels of visibility, accountability, efficiencies, collaboration, and trust.

- Bringing blockchain to life in a way that benefits companies and consumers will likely take years of trial and error. It's the "error" part that has many supply chain managers and decision-makers nervous.

- Strategy, not technology, needs to drive the business decisions, but you can't develop a sound strategy around blockchain without understanding the technology and how it applies in practical, beneficial ways to real supply chain problems.

- Leaders are interested and engaged when it comes to blockchain, but many don't have a strategy, a roadmap, or resources allocated towards creating a solution.

- Piloting blockchain almost always provides greater visibility. The question then becomes, what do you do with it?

- This book will help decision-makers at all levels of supply chain management understand blockchain and, more importantly, evaluate the value proposition the technology brings, or doesn't bring, to their work. Then it will guide you through the essential processes for making informed, practical, timely and business-savvy decisions about how – or if – you can effectively incorporate blockchain into your systems and processes.

References

Branch, J and Lopez, E (2018) 11 Technologies Set to Shape Smart Manufacturing, *Supply Chain Dive*, 21 May. www.supplychaindive.com /news/11-technologies-set-to-shape-smart-manufacturing/523576/ (archived at perma.cc/HW9G-NDC2)

Casey, M (2017) How Blockchains Will Turn Supply Chains Into Demand Chains, *Coindesk.com*, 3 November. www.coindesk.com/blockchains-will-turn-supply-chains-demand-chains/ (archived at perma.cc/RST4-QDX8)

Geiger, C (2018) Interview with the authors for this book, 22 August

Iansiti, M and Lakhani, K (2017) The Truth About Blockchain, *Harvard Business Review*, January–February. hbr.org/2017/01/the-truth-about-blockchain (archived at perma.cc/9V6P-4ZAF)

Lothian, P (2017) Interview with the authors for this book, 22 September

MHI/Deloitte (2018) The 2018 MHI Annual Industry Report – Overcoming Barriers to NextGen Supply Chain Innovation, *MHI/Deloitte*. www.mhi.org/publications/report (archived at perma.cc/V6SK-B4LG)

White, M (2018) Interview with the authors for this book, 28 August

Yiannas, F (2017) Interview with the authors for this book, 22 December

Zhao, W (2018) FedEx CEO: Adopt New Tech Like Blockchain or Be Disrupted, *Coindesk.com*, 14 May. www.coindesk.com/fedex-ceo-adopt-new-tech-like-blockchain-or-be-disrupted/ (archived at perma.cc/328K-8M3E)

PART ONE
Linking blockchain to supply networks

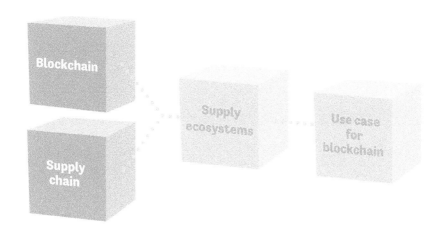

Blocked and loaded 02

The temptation is to launch any discussion involving blockchain by answering the obvious question: *What is blockchain?* The technology you end up using in your supply networks, however, might not even be blockchain, at least not in its original form. More like an illegitimate second cousin twice removed.

So, why bother defining blockchain? Because to understand that cousin – what it is or what it might be – the best place to start is by understanding its origins and its evolution. And its origins, of course, take you back to blockchain.

Defining blockchain, however, is no simple task, because there's no fully agreed-upon definition. The word wasn't coined (so to speak) until 2011. As of early 2018, the Oxford Dictionaries and Google Dictionary both had an entry for the word that was specific to blockchain's use with cryptocurrencies. The Cambridge Dictionary added an entry later in 2018 that also was specific to cryptocurrency, while Merriam-Webster added an entry that was more general but still focused on financial transactions.

Most definitions you'll find have some common elements, but each seems to take a slightly different focus. Some are pretty simple and straightforward, but they don't really tell you much about what blockchain does. Others only describe what it does, not what it is. IBM defines it as a "shared, immutable ledger for recording the history of transactions" (IBM, 2018), while SAP calls it "a reliable, difficult-to-hack record of transactions – and of who owns what" (SAP, 2018). Those are great, but for a broad definition, we're partial to Zach Steelman, an assistant professor of information systems in the Walton College of Business at the University of Arkansas. He defines blockchain as "a distributed database backed by cryptography that has consensus mechanisms to agree on when it's distributed".

Those are all pretty concise, but deeper descriptions of what blockchain does and how it works can quickly turn complicated. One blogger, for instance, promised a simple explanation of blockchain in an article with the sub-title, "The ultimate 3,500-word guide in plain English to understand Blockchain" (Mamoria, 2017). This begs the obvious question: if it takes 3,500 words to explain it, can you really call it simple?

Within all the common explanations you'll find about blockchain are a whole bunch of mind-numbing terms, many of them accompanied by mind-numbing acronyms that further confuse the issue. The various experts and developers, meanwhile, all have their preferred jargon. You'll see terms, for instance, such as distributed ledger technology (DLT), shared ledger technology (SLT), public ledger technology (PLT), Blockchain as a Service (BaaS), decentralized database, immutable ledger, trustless trust, nodes, gas prices, miners, hashes, crypto-signatures and platforms. We'll use some of those terms out of necessity, but we promise to do so in the least mind-numbing way we can.

It's hard to avoid the techno-jargon, because, when you boil it down, here's what blockchain really is: code. That makes it geek food. No one but coders really understands what it is, and they apparently need least 3,500 words to explain it. That's OK. No one but the geeks knows what the Cloud really is or what the internet really is. But the mere mortals among us know what the Cloud and the internet do for us. We know how to use them to suit our various purposes, and that's enough.

Organizations with competent information systems departments should lean into their expertise when evaluating the potential uses of blockchain and how to execute them. Others may need to hire outside experts if and when the time comes to build the technical aspects of a test case. But here's what they'll all tell you: the technology is the easy part. That means you, as a supply chain leader, get the hard part – figuring out if and how to use the technology wisely in your business. And to do that, you first need a basic understanding of what the technology can do for supply chains. Thankfully, anyone can learn what blockchain technology does and, perhaps more importantly, what it and its hybrid illegitimate cousins have the potential to do for supply networks. That's what matters, so that's how we'll approach it.

When it comes to supply networks, we define blockchain as a technology platform that establishes secured and trustworthy visibility into a database of transactions between multiple participants. It can create a transparent supply chain, because it allows for an encrypted, shared database that stores and verifies transactions, records, and just about anything digital you want that's related to the supply chain process. And unlike most existing options, it goes beyond one-on-one, point-to-point connections and can be used by entire supply chain ecosystems.

The chain of events

Blockchain's short history and meteoric rise to fame originated with the development of bitcoin, the encrypted cybercurrency that has no centralized administrator (like a government or bank). An unidentified person or group using the name *Satoshi Nakamoto* released the open-source software for bitcoins in 2009, and one of the fundamental features was, and is, blockchains.

For bitcoin to work, its masterminds needed secure, verifiable transactions that everyone using the currency could trust – even if the users who traded in the currency didn't know or trust each other. So, they develop a public digital ledger that could track, verify and record every interaction into encrypted blocks that couldn't be changed or deleted. The transactions are verified by independent users (known as nodes, which often are computers running sophisticated programs) that reach a consensus partly by solving complicated maths problems.

As you can see, blockchain isn't your grandparents' ledger. In its basic form, it's distinct in at least six significant ways. We'll take a quick look at each, both in the context of the classic, cryptocurrency version and as it relates to the emerging options that are more suited to supply networks.

First, it's decentralized ... and centralized. No single user or group of users controls a blockchain platform. The information isn't stored on any one mainframe; instead, it's stored on the Cloud. Microsoft, for instance, has more than a hundred data centres in nearly 40 regions across the globe for Azure, its Cloud computing platform that supports blockchains. Nearly 60 per cent of executives surveyed for the

2018 NHI Annual Industry Report say their organizations have already adopted Cloud computing and storage, and that figure is expected to rise to 90 per cent by 2023.

Public blockchains, the version that originated with bitcoin, have no owner, but permissioned blockchains have shared ownership among partnering organizations. The data are still stored on the Cloud, but these private or semi-private blockchains can have pre-established controls and limits. That leads some purists to argue that they aren't actually blockchains.

"There's really two different mindsets," Steelman told us. "The people who started in the blockchain space, the crypto-kiddies, as they call them, they want decentralized, completely public-accessible blockchain. That works in certain use cases, like with money, where you want to transfer with anyone. But in situations where you need private information, like a supplier–vendor relationship, that just simply doesn't work. And it will never work. Because suppliers shouldn't be able to see their competitors' prices" (Steelman, 2018).

Permissioned blockchains, once set up and running, can't be controlled or manipulated by any user without the other users knowing, which is one of the elements that creates trust among the parties. But, as Steelman pointed out, "Somebody still has to write the frontend programming and the integration with the existing systems. It's just a database, but somebody has to build all of that. But once it's up and running, it runs just as a web server. For the most part, from a technical standpoint, it runs fairly easily" (Steelman, 2018).

Not only does someone need to set it up, but someone has to govern the system. Paul Chang, a blockchain expert with IBM, put it this way during a regional Council of Supply Chain Management Professionals (CSCMP) conference we attended in 2018: "Simply because it is distributed and decentralized does not mean it is self-managing." Thus, the participants have to agree on who will do things like:

- add or delete an account;
- add or delete a participating organization;
- define and manage the permission levels;
- deploy and upgrade smart contracts on the network;

- add nodes – the computers or participants that verify data that's added to the blockchain;
- manage upgrades to the system.

So, you might reasonably ask, can a system be "decentralized" and "governed" at the same time? The key is that governance doesn't equal control. All the participants have insight into the actions that are taken and, when needed, there must be consensus for some actions.

Second, it's distributed. Information on a blockchain is shared with all of the permissioned users. When a new block is created and confirmed as authentic, the information is automatically available to everyone on that blockchain. Thus, it's distributed in a peer-to-peer fashion. Public blockchains are open to everyone. Permissioned blockchains come with mutually agreed-upon restrictions that determine which parties can add and/or view which transactions.

Third, the transactions in the ledger are validated. Each block is a record of a transaction or series of transactions that is linked to the previous block using a randomly generated cryptographic hash ID – a unique code of 64 digits. The hash ID appears in the header of a block and it identifies the content within the block.

So, let's say your production facility manufactures a batch of widgets and you create a document that describes all the relevant details about that batch. When you put that document into a block on a blockchain, the block is assigned a random hash ID. The next block in the chain might have documentation about where and how that batch of widgets is shipped out of the factory. This new block also gets a unique ID, and that ID is linked to the ID of the previous block. The blockchain programming verifies the authenticity of a block by scanning the information in the block and matching the content to the existing hash ID. Any change to the content in a block – even the removal of a single comma in the text of, say, the full manuscript of *War and Peace* – would trigger the generation of an entirely new hash ID. Thus, the system no longer would verify the comma-less version as an authentic link in the chain.

The actual verification process takes very little time, but cryptocurrencies also use a process known as "mining". The computers across the blockchain network (nodes, as the techies call them) work to solve a complex mathematical problem as part of the proof that the transactions were correctly validated. These miners are incentivized by payments (in cryptocurrency) based on the speed and accuracy of their work. Once confirmed, that "proof of work" (or "computational consensus") validates a transaction as the next block in a particular chain. This works great when users who don't know each other are involved in a transaction. Rather than trusting each other (or waiting on a third party like a bank to verify their transaction), they can trust the mathematical consensus of the blockchain.

Permissioned blockchains, which are most common in pilots involving supply networks, seldom have a need for that level of computational consensus. They typically involve a limited number of users who know each other and who have agreed on other ways to validate transactions. The simplest permissioned blockchains for supply networks, for instance, might only use peer-to-peer validations – each user's digital sign-off on a new block in the chain. Using "known users" to verify transactions is often referred to as "selective endorsement". These known users can be people, but they also can take the form of technology – for instance, a device that scans and/ or photographs received inventory.

This is one area where IoT devices may interact with (or supplant) blockchains. For instance, the Internet of Things Alliance (IOTA) provides what's known as a "tangle platform" for smart transactions between IoT devices.

"If you look at IOTA, it's not a chain," Steelman said. "Instead of everyone validating, there's a subset of validation that's based on that tree. You don't need a million people validating one little transaction if it's just a local network. With the Internet of Things, say there are five sensors in your equipment. They could validate themselves rather than having to validate against the millions and millions of other Internet of Things devices, which just wouldn't be efficient" (Steelman, 2018).

The IoT, of course, is much like blockchain when it comes to adoption within supply networks, with very few organizations using it but a great many leaders looking into it.

As a supply network increases in users and complexity, it will likely use a modified computational consensus that designates, by agreement, how the different parties verify transactions and provide proof of work. The users (or their computer nodes) may or may not have permission to see the data within the transactions, but they don't need to see them to confirm that they're valid. So, for instance, a large retailer might partner with multiple suppliers and their manufacturers to create and maintain a blockchain. Every user could take part in the consensus process, regardless of whether every user can see the actual information on the blockchain. Users (or their computers) need only solve the maths problems to assist with consensus. Sharing the consensus responsibilities adds to the trust and prevents individual players from assuming power or control over the others.

"From a consensus perspective, it's more about protecting everyone in the network," Steelman said. "What if the major retailer becomes the bad guy and decides to change transactions and there's only one other person validating the transactions? If I'm the supplier, then it's me against the big retailer. When the process is spread across everybody, then everybody is validating everybody else and protecting everybody else, even though they may not know them. It's a self-imposed, trust monitoring system where one party, even the major player, can't do something against one person or the group without everyone seeing that something's up" (Steelman, 2018).

This type of trust from the validation process helps give blockchain an edge over existing databases. "Blockchain makes the process go smoother because there is built-in trust where, for instance, vendors aren't having to trust the big retailer and their programmers to make sure all the systems are integrated," Steelman said. "The system itself creates some of that trust. If you have an iffy situation or relationship, blockchain can make it better. But it's not guaranteed to make it better, because somebody still has to write that code" (Steelman, 2018).

Fourth, every user has a unique digital key. Much like the hash ID, this is a randomly generated alphanumeric code, but this one serves as a user's password to access the system. In the cryptocurrency world, it's the key that allows access to your digital wallet and ensures that only you have access to the funds in that wallet. The key allows you to decrypt the data within a block that you created. If you lose that key on a public blockchain, however, you lose access to everything. There's no one in customer service to call or e-mail who can resend it to you or reset it for you, because there's no central authority. Permissioned blockchains used by businesses can require multiple signatures to approve major transactions before they are added to the blockchain.

Fifth, the information recorded is immutable. Once a block is added to the chain, the data within it are there to stay. They can't be changed or deleted. This often is referred to as the "shared state", which is computer programming lingo for agreed-upon information that the network has locked into its memory. The information in the blocks is forever linked together. The algorithms ensure that every entry in the database is permanently available in chronological order, and the hashing ensures that changes can't be made to existing blocks within a chain. Users can't create forks in the road, so everyone must travel along one shared path of truth.

A downside to this reality is that updating a blockchain's code or correcting human error isn't easy. Programmers can't change the old code or update content to fix a typo; they have to create new code or new information in new blocks that create a new link in the chain.

Many business leaders also worry about using a database that can't be deleted. This is true, but, as Steelman pointed out, the digital keys for a permissioned blockchain can be deleted and the access rights to see certain blocks can be changed. "The data will always be there," he said, "but it will be encrypted, so it may not always be accessible. All the data is hashed and protected. Remove the access to it and nobody would be able to see it" (Steelman, 2018).

Sixth, the ledger is governed by programmed logic. This allows for smart contracts, which are one of the driving forces behind block-chain applications across supply networks. Smart contracts are simply business agreements embedded in the database that execute auto-matically with the appropriate transactions. Users can set up unique rules and algorithms that trigger transactions or implications and allow the validation to happen through coding within the system. For instance, a blockchain network might be programmed to issue an invoice (a new block) that triggers a payment (another new block) whenever it verifies that a product has reached its destination (another new block). Or it might allow for automated reverse auctions, where a buyer simply enters the criteria for what it needs, the computers of competing vendors respond automatically, and a winning bid is selected – all in a matter of minutes and with no human interactions.

"Blockchain works well for small breakdowns of things that are repetitive and can be very well defined," Steelman said. "If you can define each attribute based on the bids that come in, you could set up a smart contract to automatically trigger certain actions. That's the biggest piece of smart contracts – the executable pieces of code based on events or triggers. It's just an 'if/then' algorithm" (Steelman, 2018).

The open access of multiple users combined with the encrypted programming and validated results all potentially work together to create the equivalent of triple-entry, tamper-proof bookkeeping. And, most importantly, this type of bookkeeping has applications far beyond cryptocurrency or even the financial industry. Don Tapscott, co-author of *Blockchain Revolution*, put it this way: blockchain is "an incorruptible digital ledger of economic transactions that can be programmed to record not just financial transactions but virtually everything of value and importance to humankind" (Tapscott and Tapscott, 2015).

Summary: six distinctives of blockchain

- It's decentralized... and centralized.
- It's distributed.
- The transactions in the ledger are validated.
- Every user has a unique digital key.
- The information recorded is immutable.
- The ledger is governed by programmed logic.

Using blockchain to show your roots

One of the questions we often hear from supply chain professionals goes something like this: "What's the functional process for using blockchain? In other words, what does it look like to actually use it in our business?"

If you boil it down to the four most basic steps, a permissioned blockchain would look like this:

Step 1: Someone signs into their account online and enters a transaction, which includes contracts, records, or other digital information about an asset.

Step 2: The transaction is shared throughout the network of computers that have been assigned to receive it.

Step 3: The network of computers validate the transaction, including the user's status, using algorithms. Verification occurs when the computers (nodes) reach consensus.

Step 4: When verification occurs, the transaction becomes a block in the digital ledger and is permanently available to all authorized participants and cannot be edited or deleted.

By late 2017, a good number of entities were exploring the use of blockchain as a means for adding value to their supply networks – everyone from retailers like Walmart and suppliers like Unilever to logistics startups like ShipChain and countries like the government of Singapore. In 2018, an increasing number of logistics-related companies joined the party. In most cases, nothing had moved past the pilot stage. But one of the few full-fledged early adopters of the technology within its supply chain was the Grass Roots Farmers' Cooperative. And it provides a simple illustration of how blockchain actually functions to create a transparent supply chain.

Grass Roots has a modest supply chain – truly more of a chain than a network. The member farmers raise premium non-GMO chickens, turkeys, cattle and pigs, which they sell to the cooperative. The meats typically are processed at Natural State Processing, a plant owned in part by the co-op, and then are sold by the co-op through its e-commerce site or to wholesalers, who sell to grocery stores or restaurants around the United States. Here's how Grass Roots uses blockchain in an example with one of its chicken farmers.

The farmer uses a smartphone or desktop application to log into an online platform and register a batch of chickens in the system. The farmer enters data about things like the quantity (usually 800 to 2,000), the batch number and the farm number. This "genesis" block on the chain can include digital copies of supporting paperwork, and it is finalized when the system generates its 30-character digital hash ID. Now anyone with access to the platform can log in, see it, and, if authorized, add a new block to the chain. But no one can change the information in the genesis block without creating an entirely different hash ID and, therefore, an entirely new chain.

When that batch of chickens is sent to the processing plant, the farmer and the processing plant both sign in and formally accept the transfer of the assets, which confirms the transaction and creates the second block with a digital ID that links it to the genesis block. The chickens are processed, packaged and cased, and each package and case are labelled with a QR code and short URL address that identifies it as part of that specific batch. The cases are transferred to Grass Roots. After Grass Roots and the processing plant formally accept the transfer (another peer-to-peer confirmation), another new block with another unique ID is confirmed and joins the chain. A block is also created for cases that are transferred to a wholesaler, as well as for cases that end up in a retail store.

Figure 2.1 shows how it might look.

By scanning the QR code or entering the URL, anyone can see all the information in this blockchain. A salesperson for the wholesaler, for instance, might use a smartphone or tablet to scan a sample case when showing the product to a buyer at a restaurant in California. A customer, meanwhile, might scan it in the grocery store or look it up on a home computer.

At first, Grass Roots was only using the blockchain to show the transfer of assets. But it was working on plans to add additional information – things like certifications, purchase orders for the non-GMO livestock feed, and information about pricing and profit-margins at each stage in the process.

Some suppliers within the diamond industry, another early adopter, use a similar process to authenticate the quality and source of diamonds. Blockchains, however, get more complicated and more potential problems and risks arise when they are used in more complex, multi-tier supply networks. A laptop, for instance, consists of thousands of parts that come from a variety of suppliers who themselves all have a variety of suppliers, many of whom also have their own suppliers. Many of those suppliers provide materials or parts

Figure 2.1 A visual of a blockchain

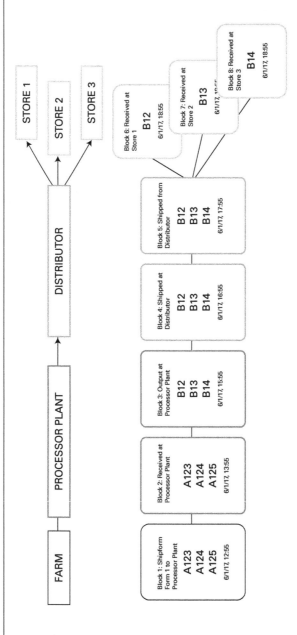

for laptop producers who compete against each other. The materials and parts are moved from one point to another by a variety of methods – trucks, trains, ships, aeroplanes and more trucks. Aligning every player on that type of shared blockchain platform is no easy task. Still, blockchain advocates predict it will happen – eventually. And, in some cases, it's very close.

Where can I buy some blocks?

As blockchain makes its way into the marketplace, there's no shortage of companies vying for space at the table. Most, if not all, are operating from one of three platforms – Hyperledger, Ethereum or Corda.

Ethereum is a public blockchain that's very similar to bitcoin but with features more compatible with business uses. It operates with its own currency, the Ether, and you have to use Ether to run a transaction. Because it's public and based on a cryptocurrency, you have to pay small fees to build a platform. These fees reward for the miners for their work in validating new blocks that are added to the chain.

Hyperledger, meanwhile, is an open-source blockchain technology that launched in 2016 with 30 founding members that included Accenture, Cisco, IBM and Intel. The Hyperledger Project is run by The Linux Foundation, a non-profit organization that most companies recognize, respect and trust. In less than two years, the project had grown to around two hundred corporate and associate members, including a diverse governing board of 21 members.

When Apache Software Foundation co-founder Brian Behlendorf took the role of executive director for Hyperledger in May 2016, he quickly made it clear that the vision for the project was to become a "business blockchain umbrella" (Behlendorf, 2016). You don't need a coin to run a transaction, because the incentives for mining are based on each user's investment into the success of the database. One Network and many other for-profit companies are building their blockchain solutions using Hyperledger, which already has several distinct business frameworks with names like Burrow, Indy, Iroha, Fabric and Sawtooth, as well as programming tools like Cello, Composer, Explorer, and Quilt.

Corda is an open-source blockchain project created by R3, an enterprise software company that's partnering with banks and other financial-related institutions.

Most of the world's top technology and software companies are offering blockchain-based solutions in some form or fashion. Amazon and Azure (Microsoft's Cloud service) both allow you to spin up a blockchain service on their Cloud platform regardless of whether it uses Hyperledger, Ethereum or Corda. Oracle, SAP and Salesforce have blockchain initiatives. Microsoft partners with EY, Accenture and Consensys for strategic consulting and implementation related to blockchain. IBM and SAP both provide a combination of consulting and hosting options, and sometimes even work in partnership with each other. Marie Wieck, the general manager of IBM's blockchain division, explained IBM's approach in an interview with *Forbes* contributor Jason Bloomberg: "We're focusing on permissioned blockchain with modular components. The goal is enterprise-grade productivity" (Bloomberg, 2018).

The advantage of known players like Microsoft, IBM and SAP is that they bring decades of expertise in both the technology and supply chain logistics, they have experience across industries and across borders, and they are well positioned to standardize and scale the technology as it matures. A disadvantage is that these companies typically are in the business of creating proprietary platforms that may not always operate well with competing platforms.

Startups, on the other hand, are typically nimbler, better positioned to provide hands-on service to smaller companies, and less likely to get caught in the "hybrid trap" (Suarez *et al*, 2018). Instead of trying to build hybrid models that work with existing systems (the common tactic among established companies), the startups can disrupt with entirely new models that aren't hindered by legacy systems.

Historically, one or more startups emerge as market leaders, leaving the established companies with hybrid models that are in danger of irrelevance. The lack of barriers to entry, however, has allowed for a crowded field of entrepreneurial competition, and many of the blockchain startups have played on the hype to overstate their credibility. So, while many of these startups are legit contenders,

Table 2.1 Advantages of blockchain providers

Advantages of blockchain providers		
	Old guard	**New guard**
Greater technology experience	✓	
Greater supply chain/logistics experience	✓	
More experience across industries	✓	
More international experience	✓	
Greater ability to standardize	✓	
Better suited to scale	✓	
Operates more nimbly		✓
More hands-on with smaller companies		✓
More willing to disrupt		✓

others are wolves in sheep's clothing. The lesson: *caveat emptor* ("let the buyer beware") never goes out of fashion.

As we'll discuss later, this makes selecting the right technology partner critical for setting up and implementing a supply chain use case.

Regardless of the platforms for using blockchain or for all the whiz-bang bells and whistles those platforms claim they will deliver, the question remains for supply chain professionals: Will this really work? That's where understanding the hype comes in.

Chain links: Key points from this chapter

- Blockchain is a distributed database backed by cryptography that has consensus mechanisms to agree on when it's distributed.

- The technology involved with blockchain isn't difficult for IT professionals. That means supply chain leaders get the hard part of figuring out if and how to use the technology wisely.

- For supply chain professionals, blockchain is a technology platform that establishes secured and trustworthy visibility into a database of transactions between multiple participants. It can create a transparent supply chain, because it allows for an encrypted, shared database that stores and verifies transactions, records, and just about anything digital you want that's related to the supply chain process.

- Blockchain is distinct in at least six significant ways: it's decentralized, it's distributed, transactions are validated, users have a unique digital key, the records are immutable, the ledger is governed by programmed logic.

- Most blockchains operate from one of three platforms – Hyperledger, Ethereum or Corda.

References

Behlendorf, B (2016) Meet Hyperledger: An 'Umbrella' for Open Source Blockchain & Smart Contract Technologies [Blog] *hyperledger.org*, 13 September. hyperledger.org/blog/2016/09/13/meet-hyperledger-an-umbrella-for-open-source-blockchain-smart-contract-technologies (archived at perma.cc/M2DV-RBZF)

Bloomberg, J (2018) IBM Bets Company on Exponential Innovation in AI, Blockchain, and Quantum Computing, *Forbes.com*. www.forbes.com/sites/jasonbloomberg/2018/03/22/ibm-bets-company-on-exponential-innovation-in-ai-blockchain-and-quantum-computing/#78560c173ea2 (archived at perma.cc/ZT4G-VMEB)

IBM (2018) Welcome to IBM Blockchain, *IBM*. www.ibm.com/myibm/hightech (archived at perma.cc/6G3G-2KUN)

Mamoria, M. (2017) WTF is the Blockchain? The Ultimate 3,500-Word Guide in Plain English to Understand Blockchain, *hackernoon.com*, 30

June. https://hackernoon.com/wtf-is-the-blockchain-1da89ba19348 (archived at perma.cc/VBK4-MYXY)

SAP (2018) What Is Blockchain?, *SAP* www.sap.com/products/leonardo/blockchain/what-is-blockchain.html (archived at perma.cc/EH2Y-27YU)

Steelman, Z (2018) Interview with the authors for this book, 2 February

Suarez, F *et al* (2018) The Hybrid Trap: Why Most Efforts to Bridge Old and New Technology Miss the Mark, *MIT Sloan Management Review*, 5 March. https://sloanreview.mit.edu/article/the-hybrid-trap-why-most-efforts-to-bridge-old-and-new-technology-miss-the-mark/ (archived at perma.cc/G96R-UYR6)

Tapscott, D and Tapscott, A (2015) SXSW Preview: What's the Next Generation Internet? Surprise: It's all about the Blockchain! [LinkedIn article], *linkedin.com*, 12 March. www.linkedin.com/pulse/whats-next-generation-internet-surprise-its-all-don-tapscott (archived at perma.cc/R5L3-ENGV)

The power
of hype

03

There's something about blockchain technology that causes many supply chain leaders to hold their hands up stop-sign style and say: "Pump the brakes a little, would you? This all sounds a bit familiar. And a bit too good to be true." We understand.

We inevitably experience a bit of *déjà vu* whenever we visit, or read articles by, the most passionate apostles of blockchain technology. One research paper called blockchain a "revolutionary technology" with "cutting-edge applications". Another predicted it would "profoundly impact the nature of companies in general". Yet another called it "a novel solution to the age-old human problem of trust" that "could be the most consequential development in information technology since the internet".

Such predictions can sound eerily familiar. The only difference often is that the word *blockchain* has replaced some other technological innovation – radio-frequency identification (RFID), the Cloud, electronic data interchange (EDI) or the Internet of Things (IoT), for instance.

Many of the other technologies that came with a promise of changing the supply chain world indeed added value. We're not discounting the relevance of RFID, the Cloud, EDI or IoT, but they haven't created a seismic shift in the way supply chains function. Rather than changing the supply chain world, they changed a portion of it – and not always in the manner predicted.

There's an obvious correlation between blockchain and the hype surrounding RFID, beginning around 2003. RFID arrived with great potential, but many of its advocates were overzealous in their predictions. If you were waiting for refrigerators with RFID readers that would auto-replenish or for RFID to replace barcodes, well, you're still waiting. As we'll explore in more detail later, many such predictions have yet to come true, even if the potential is still there.

If blockchain technology lives up to its hype, however, most, if not all, of these technologies figure to grow in significance. Rather than making them obsolete, blockchain could make them more relevant. For instance, one of the issues with IoT is its ability to confirm the identity of its users, which is something blockchain promises to solve. And as management professor Nir Kshertri pointed out in an article for the *International Journal of Information Management*, technologies such as IoT, RFID tags, GPS tags and chips, and other sensors allow for "an enhanced, real-time tracking of goods from the origin", which makes them a great fit with blockchain (Kshertri, 2018).

Some technologies, of course, live up to or even surpass their hype. Consider the internet. In a September 1996 edition of *Time*, former Netscape CEO Jim Barksdale called the internet "the printing press of the technology era". And in that same article, Microsoft founder Bill Gates called it "a revolution in communications that will change the world significantly. (It) opens a whole new way to communicate with your friends and find and share information of all types. Microsoft is betting that the internet will continue to grow in popularity until it is as mainstream as the telephone is today" (Von Clausewitz, 2016).

Or consider the buzz around the iPhone. At the Macworld conference in January 2007, Apple founder Steve Jobs said, "An iPod, a phone, an internet mobile communicator... these are *not* three separate devices! And we are calling it iPhone! Today Apple is going to reinvent the phone. And here it is" (Agar, 2013).

The iPhone, indeed, was a game changer, and not just for the phone industry. And the internet, of course, truly had a revolutionary impact on our world, including the way supply networks operate. Comparisons between blockchain and the internet are a common analogy, and with good reason. The internet is an underlying technology that allows hundreds of popular applications, some useful in very practical ways and others just plain old fun. Its influence began with e-mail and has grown to include our modern cyber-driven world of blogs, websites and apps that have changed how we work, socialize, shop, play and, some would say, think. It also led to Cloud computing, which provides the technical structure for, you guessed it, blockchains. And blockchain provides the underlying technology platform for a plethora of potential applications that promise to fundamentally change the way we do business in supply chain management.

When all is said and done, supply chain decision-makers are left with a simple question: Can we believe the hype about blockchain?

The only accurate answer to that question is a big, fat "Maybe". But you aren't looking for a wishy-washy response to such an important question, so we'll tell you what we *really* think: blockchain technology absolutely will impact the way leaders, managers and consumers interact with and manage supply chains. In fact, it already is having an impact. And there is no reason to believe it can't have a game-changing impact – in time. But here's the most interesting thing, not to mention the most relevant for supply chain leaders: the hype of blockchain – even more so than the technology itself – already is radically influencing the future of supply chain management all across the globe.

Just a database

New Zealand's temperate climate and regular rainfall help create ideal conditions for year-round green pastures that feed the country's dairy cows. The herds produce fresh milk, some of which is processed into cheese, milk powder or milk fat. And some of that milk fat is shipped across the Pacific Ocean to a factory in Pennsylvania.

Cocoa beans, meanwhile, mostly from family-run farms in South America and western Africa, also find their way to this Pennsylvania factory, as does non-fat milk powder from California, peanuts from farms across the southern United States and sugar beets sourced from 11 different states.

These ingredients go through unique processes at the factory and eventually come together in a glorious mixture affectionately known to the world as a Reese's Peanut Butter Cup. The chocolate-and-peanut-butter concoctions, which were first created by Harry Burnett Reese back in 1928, are then packaged and begin the next stage of their journey, stopping in warehouses en route to stores all over the world before ending up in the mouths of sweet-toothed consumers.

That's the overly simplified version of one product's supply network. But imagine if every detail involved in that product's journey to the marketplace could be loaded into a highly secured database and shared with everyone from the farmers to the logistics companies to the managers at the factory, warehouses and stores, and even to the consumers – anyone with an interest in seeing it and a need for using it.

What if this database allowed access to documented proof of every transfer of ownership in the process, both for the raw ingredients that were sourced and for the product as it moved from the factory to the stores?

What if consumers could peer into the database and see timestamped videos, photographs and documentation that traced the milk fat from the dairy farms in New Zealand to the candy factory in Hershey, Penn., verifying, among other things, that it came from grass-fed cows? And what if those customers could see proof that the workers in the cocoa fields of Peru were paid a fair wage?

What if the manufacturer and its suppliers could use the database to analyse sales trends, more accurately forecast demand, and thereby better manage inventories and decrease the bullwhip effect?

What if procurement teams could use the data for more transparent negotiations, and the systems for more highly automated management of purchase orders, payments and invoices?

What if shipping companies could use the database to instantly process digitized legal documents and transfer ownership at the shipyard, reducing the paper in the paperwork and the time containers spent waiting to move from the dock to a train or truck and on to the factory?

What if retailers and the government could instantly trace any ingredient back to a specific farm to zero in on the source of a foodborne illness? Or verify regulatory compliance?

And what if this database was programmed to trigger and record new transactions and payments when specific conditions were met at specific times during the supply chain process?

We know what you're thinking: *Those are the promises of blockchain!*

In fact, when you line up the promises of blockchain for supply chain management, they align pretty closely with what you'd want from an ideal supply chain. And, for what it's worth, they also align pretty closely with the lessons from Robert Fulghum's classic book, *All I Really Need to Know I Learned in Kindergarten.* In other words, you can complicate it if you want, but it's really pretty basic stuff.

The ideal supply chain provides the right scope, which is acted upon by the right capabilities, which leads to the right results. So, when we think of the ideal supply chain, we categorize its critical characteristics in terms of scope, capabilities or results. And when we look at the promises of blockchain through a supply chain filter, those promises also should fit in those categories.

For the most part, they do. Check it out (Table 3.1).

Table 3.1   Blockchain and the ideal supply chain

All I Really Need to Know I Learned in Kindergarten – Robert Fulghum	Ideal Supply Chain s = scope c = capabilities r = results	Blockchain Promises
1. Share everything.	Visibility (c)	Distributed, decentralized, multiple players
2. Play fair.	Collaboration (c), reliable (r)	Trustless trust (shared processes and record-keeping)
3. Don't hit people.	Ethical (r)	Immutability
4. Put things back where you found them.	Business alignment (c)	Documents transfer of ownership
5. CLEAN UP YOUR OWN MESS.	Sustainable (r)	Inherent accountability
6. Don't take things that aren't yours.	International (s), cross-functional (s), cross-company (s), segmented (c)	Secured by cryptography

Table 3.1 *continued*

All I Really Need to Know I Learned in Kindergarten– Robert Fulghum	Ideal Supply Chain s = scope c = capabilities r = results	Blockchain Promises
7. Say you're SORRY when you HURT somebody.	Traceability (c)	Traceability
8. Wash your hands before you eat.	Integration (c)	One version of shared truth.
9. Flush.	Efficient (c), real-time speed (r)	Speed (transactions are near instantaneous)
10. Warm cookies and cold milk are good for you.	Customer-centric (c)	Serves the needs of the marketplace
11. Live a balanced life – learn some and drink some and draw some and paint some and sing and dance and play and work every day some.	Integration (c)	Immutability
12. Take a nap every afternoon.	Adaptive (c)	Agile, creates efficiencies; reduces overheads and the need for intermediaries
13. When you go out into the world, watch out for traffic, hold hands, and stick together.	Resilient (r)	Interoperability
14. Be aware of wonder. Remember the little seed in the Styrofoam cup: The roots go down and the plant goes up and nobody really knows how or why, but we are all like that.	Agile/responsive (r)	Programmable

Table 3.1 *continued*

All I Really Need to Know I Learned in Kindergarten – Robert Fulghum	Ideal Supply Chain s = scope c = capabilities r = results	Blockchain Promises
15. Goldfish and hamster and white mice and even the little seed in the Styrofoam cup – they all die. So do we.	Predictability (c)	Predictable
16. And then remember the Dick-and-Jane books and the first word you learned – the biggest word of all – "LOOK".	Information rich (c)	Visibility

At this point you might be having a euphoric moment. Supply chain nirvana is on the horizon! Well, guess what: you don't need blockchain to accomplish any of those things. Not one.

Zach Steelman, an assistant professor of information systems in the Walton College of Business at the University of Arkansas, is an expert on the technical aspects of blockchain technology. His research confirms what we've learned at every turn when working on this book: blockchain – at least when it comes to applications for supply chain professionals – is really just the next stage in the evolution of database technologies. "I view blockchain very fundamentally as a distributed database backed by cryptography," Steelman told us. "Period. It's just a database that has consensus mechanisms to agree on when it's distributed. ... The core pieces have been around since the 1960s and 70s – distributed databases and cryptography – they just didn't put them together in this format until the late 2000s" (Steelman, 2018).

That's why, when you dig into the solutions offered to businesses under the broad umbrella of blockchain, you might find yourself saying something like, "We could do that with a database". You could create a chain of blocks on a database. You could program a database to execute a smart contract. You could trace a product to its origin using a database. You *could* do most everything blockchain offers to the supply chain world by using existing database technologies.

Even one of blockchain's most ardent advocates – a solutions specialist for IBM who has worked on multiple blockchain pilots – won't argue this point. "There's some fundamental technical differences between blockchain and historic, classic technology," Jeffrey Keller told us, "but I think, in concept, certainly with code and database you can do many of the same things" (Keller, 2018).

But here's the reality: you're not doing it – at least not at a widespread scale that's moving the needle towards more efficient supply networks.

Think about something like cleaning up a master database. As one leader told us, that's a job no one wants to do and that tends to list its permanent address as "backburner". But to use blockchain effectively, you'll need that database cleaned up. So, what should have been a priority actually becomes a priority, and it gets done. In fact, we'll tell you over and over that adding blockchain to broken processes and systems won't fix the broken processes and systems. All that gives you is broken processes and systems that are automated. And entering flawed data into a blockchain platform won't sanitize the data. The garbage you put in will stink just as much when it comes out. And if you don't have access to the right information from the right partners using the same standards, the insights from the database will be incomplete or downright wrong. As a representative of a technology company put it during one of the conferences we hosted, we could solve all these problems with a relational database – if you forced everyone to participate. If everyone would participate, and if everyone would align on the same standards, and if....

The supply chain world has long known that it needs trustworthy collaboration between partners, real-time data, alignment on key standards, greater visibility, faster traceability and all of the other bells and whistles that are hyped by blockchain. And existing database technologies can do much of that. But the supply chain world isn't doing it, largely because supply networks consist of dozens upon dozens of separate organizations with different and sometimes competing agendas. They work together and depend upon one another, but have seldom reached consensus on how to collaborate for everyone's common good. Data, which at times are still printed or even hand-written rather than digital, tend to travel in linear fashion from one partner to the next, where they're recast into a different system with different standards until they're transferred again to the next partner. The modern, global supply chain, in fact, often can be summed up in one word: fragmented.

Blockchain's biggest benefit to business, therefore, isn't what it will do that we couldn't do before – although it definitely enables some important innovations and efficiencies – but that it is pushing and pulling the supply chain world towards innovations it should have implemented over the past 20 years. Blockchain is forcing many potential users to fix their broken processes and systems, to clean up their data, and to work in and across industries to create shared solutions for the common good. When you get right down to it, that's the biggest reason blockchain matters to supply chain professionals – because the hype around the technology is causing an inescapable sea change across all facets of supply networks.

RevUnit, a technology design company based in our area, picked up on this pretty quickly as it began exploring the potential of blockchain for its clients. Spruce Feinstein, a software architect at RevUnit, pointed out that "...technologies making up blockchain [are] really interesting, but not as novel as the hype indicates". But he quickly added, "we already see blockchain acting as a catalyst that is forcing organizations and consumers to think... about transparency and data sharing. Those conversations and agreements have the potential to drive significant disruption in many industries" (Feinstein, 2018).

Blockchain, in the context of supply networks, isn't disruptive but the buzz around it is. The hype, in ways unlike the buzz surrounding any previous technologies, is driving unprecedented investments across multiple industries. Research by Mary Lacity, Director of the Blockchain Center of Excellence at the University of Arkansas and author of *A Manager's Guide to Blockchains for Business*, found that by early 2018, corporations had invested around $1.2 billion in blockchain technology. Professional services companies like IBM, SAP and Microsoft had invested another $1 billion. And venture capitalists had poured some $4 billion into startups connected to blockchains.

Gartner, a US-based technology research firm, predicts the widespread investments into blockchain will cause the "business value-add of blockchain" to grow to "slightly more than $176 billion by 2025, and then it will exceed $3.1 trillion by 2030" (Lovelock *et al*, 2017).

Those types of investments are one reason executives and experts in IT sectors predict 10 per cent of global gross domestic product (GDP) will be stored on blockchain technology as soon as 2025 (World Economic Forum, 2015). All those investments aren't connected to supply chain business challenges, but they are a result of changes that have the potential for a network effect that could allow supply chain networks to align on standards and best practices. Supply networks will have undergone a significant makeover and emerged looking better – more efficient, productive, transparent, collaborative and trustworthy.

Imagine a remodelled classic car. There's a reality television show in the United States called *Gas Garage Monkey* where this guy buys classic cars, takes them to his shop in Dallas and spends thousands of dollars over several weeks stripping the cars of their inner parts and replacing them with modern parts, fancy accessories and a fresh coat of paint. The result – it's still the same car. However, it not only looks better but it's a high-performance machine that efficiently does way beyond what it originally was designed to do. All it took was the right parts, the right technicians and, most of all, a commitment to the investment.

From hype to concrete

New technologies are known to go through five basic phases when it comes to hype. Gartner came up with a commonly used graphic representation (Figure 3.1) that shows a technology trigger, a peak of inflated expectations, a trough of disillusionment, a slope of enlightenment and a plateau of productivity. The peak of inflated expectations represents the crescendo of the hype, and it fades quickly into the trough of disillusionment when the hype isn't followed by at least a few scalable success stories. If the technology has real value, it then goes through a period of renewed visibility and enlightenment about its value, followed by a "plateau of productivity".

Figure 3.1   Gartner hype curve (Gartner, 2019)

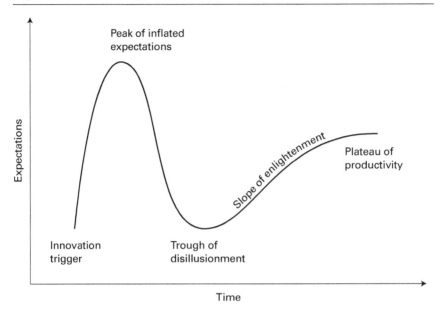

In 2018, the team at Gartner plotted more than a dozen emerging technologies on their hype curve and did some predictive analysis (see Figure 3.2). In short, Gartner believes blockchain has passed the peak of inflated expectations, is dropping into the trough of disillusionment and is 10 years away from reaching the plateau of productivity.

We have great respect for the team at Gartner and we mostly agree with their analysis. The "10 years" estimate, for instance, might be overly optimistic. But that's a minor quibble. The bigger difference in our take on blockchain hype is on where it's heading before it reaches that plateau. The hype around blockchain's potential applications to the supply chain, it seems to us, has spiked, but then actually has held steady even without any applications that have demonstrated widespread, scalable success. In other words, blockchain's hype is outrunning its proven success stories and it is defying the pattern represented in the traditional hype cycle (Figure 3.3).

Sceptics would lead you to believe that there are no successful business uses of blockchain and little hope that any are on the horizon. In fact, there are several real examples of businesses using blockchain technology in effective ways that can't be easily duplicated

Figure 3.2 Hype cycle for emerging technologies (Walker, 2018)

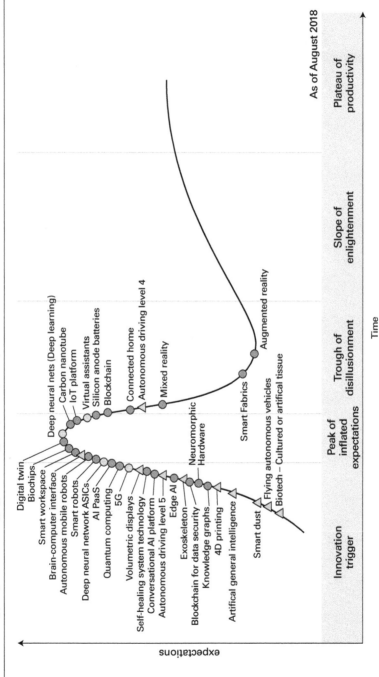

Plateau will be reached:

○ less than 2 years   ◔ 2 to 5 years   ● 5 to 10 years   △ more than 10 years   ⊗ obsolete before plateau

Figure 3.3   Our view of blockchain on the hype curve

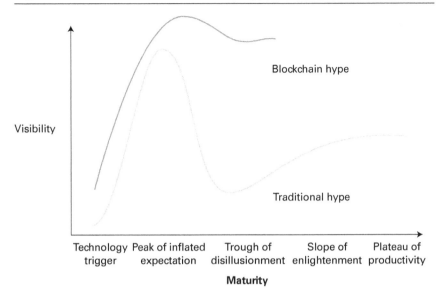

with other technologies. More importantly, as we've already noted, some of the world's largest companies are investing heavily when it comes to developing business uses for blockchain technologies. They are, in fact, the reason why the hype has gained such momentum and generally avoided, so far, the disillusionment stage.

One reason we probably see blockchain slightly differently from others is because our primary focus is on supply chain management. The broader hype around blockchain is usually connected to bitcoin or other such cryptocurrencies. So, in late 2017 through early 2019, you were beginning to hear more naysayers about blockchain's potential. *Forbes* staff writer Parmy Olson, for instance, wrote in January 2019 that blockchain, as a buzzword, had "lost its sheen" among executives. "The technology's big problem is that it doesn't scale," she wrote. "Millions of people use credit cards every day, but the original blockchain that underpinned bitcoin could only handle a few hundred credit card transactions at a time. That meant it could never go mainstream" (Olson, 2019).

Blockchain in supply chain applications, however, do not have the same constraints of scale compared to bitcoin. Bitcoin's main constraint is mostly related to mining, which rarely occurs in blockchain supply chain management applications. In supply chains, as we'll get into in more detail later, the constraints are more about scaling the network of participants (getting more suppliers on board, for instance, especially at the raw materials end of the chain).

Tech and software giants like Microsoft, IBM and SAP all are partnering with businesses, governments and, in some cases, each other to test supply chain uses for blockchain technologies. As of this writing, there are no fewer than 40 consortiums and alliances – groups like the Blockchain in Transportation Alliance (BiTA) – that are working to align their industry or multiple industries on ways to use blockchain. Dozens of venture-capital-funded startups and several logistics-related companies are also offering blockchain technology solutions or working to integrate blockchain into their supply chain services.

Here are some notable projects:

- The Port of Rotterdam helped create BlockLab, an alliance of engineers, developers and other partners that launched in 2017 to explore ways blockchain might improve the energy and logistics industries.

- The US Department of State joined a pilot in 2018 with Coca-Cola and the non-profit Blockchain Trust Accelerator that is attempting to create a secure registry of workers and their contracts to combat forced labour practices by some of the beverage company's suppliers around the world.

- The 250-plus members in the blockchain in BiTA account for more than 70% of the freight moved in the United States. BiTA was founded in August 2017 to help develop standards and provide education on blockchain in the transportation and logistics industry.

- IBM is working with several logistics industry stalwarts, including shipping giant Maersk Group and Kansas City Southern Railway.

- More than a dozen major food industry players like Walmart, Kroger, Wegmans, Discolls, Nestlé, Danone, McCormick, Dole, Unilever and Tyson Food joined with IBM to form a consortium in 2017 that began collaborating on creating effective business solutions involving blockchain technologies.

- From that, Unilever began a one-year pilot programme late in 2017 to help manage financial transactions in its tea supply chain, partnering with banks and as many as 10,000 farmers in Malawi. They hope to increase efficiencies and accuracy in tracking tea from farms to stores, building credibility among consumers who want sustainably sourced tea.

- Walmart also joined with IBM, Chinese retailer JD.com and Tsinghau University to create the Blockchain Food Safety Alliance to promote collaboration that they hope will improve food tracking in China, where consumer trust has free-fallen in recent years because of a variety of food safety scandals.

Few major corporations have done more to press blockchain initiatives than Walmart, which ran a pilot project that tracked packages of pork from farms to supermarkets in China, followed by a larger pilot that tracked sliced mangoes from farms in Mexico to stores in the United States. By the end of 2017, the global retailer was tracking around a dozen food products on the IBM Food Trust blockchain platform, and by late 2018 that number had grown to more than 30.

Walmart also has filed several patent applications related to blockchain technology, and not all of them involve food safety. In June 2018, for instance, the retailer was awarded a patent for a system that would use blockchain to store medical information. The idea is that people with certain medical risks would have a wearable device that stores their medical information. In an emergency that leaves a patient unable to communicate, first responders or other healthcare workers could access the information with an RFID scanner.

Based on other patent applications, Walmart also sees potential value in blockchain when it comes to reselling purchased products, creating "smart packages" systems for track-and-trace, and even for an electrical grid powered by cryptocurrencies. One patent application, titled "Systems, Devices, and Methods for In-Field Authenticating of Autonomous Robots", describes a blockchain-enabled system for operating drones and robots that deliver packages throughout the supply chain.

Most companies aren't filing patent applications, but they are interested in the efficiencies blockchain offers to the supply chain. Very few have moved past pilots, however, and the vast majority of supply chain professionals have far more questions than answers when it comes to blockchain. One of the reasons discussions about the technology feel so gut-wrenching is because it offers so much but comes with so many lingering questions. The hyped-up promises of blockchain are big and enticing.

Here are just a few:

- Greater transparency into the supply networks' promises to deter fraud by offering the potential for secure, trustworthy real-time access and insight into the process up and down the chain. This helps not only businesses but also consumers, because it promises greater insights into the products they're buying. UK-based Blockverify, for instance, is piloting a program that would allow medical professionals and consumers to scan medications and verify their integrity. And in the food industry, where it's estimated that more food is sold as "organic" than is actually produced, trustworthy visibility could verify such claims and increase consumer confidence and loyalty. "It seems to me that in the 21st Century, if people want to know what they're buying, how it's made, and where it's made, and where it comes from, they ought to know," said the FDA's Frank Yiannas. "I don't know why that should be secret, right? And consumers are increasingly demanding this information" (Yiannas, 2017).

- Trusted automation promises to create efficiencies that save money at every stage in a supply network. For instance, managers potentially can track products through the supply chain; share information with suppliers and other partners; track invoices and payments; verify certifications and transactions; better manage supply and demand needs, inventory, and freight transportation; solve many of their contract management issues; and offer accurate information to customers.

- A faster way to trace a product's origins promises to improve things like food safety during recalls.

- Blockchain allows for multiple users throughout a complex network, not just one-to-one or one-to-a-few users of a traditional siloed shared-information system.

- Blockchain promises the ability to track compliance issues and streamline enforcement.

The managers and executives who took part in our blockchain for supply chain workshop in 2018 referenced many of the same benefits when asked what factors are driving their consideration and adoption of blockchain in the supply chain (see Figure 3.4).

Figure 3.4   Drivers for blockchain in the supply chain

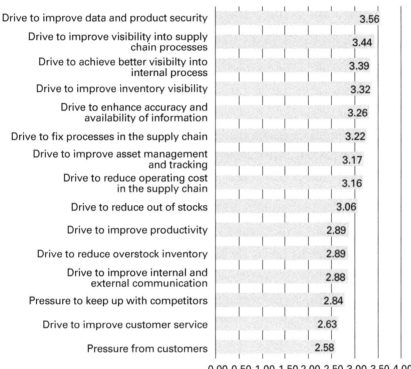

The top drivers were around transparency and visibility, and our interviews with the participants made it clear that the ultimate goal is to move towards the upper right quadrant we identified earlier – shared process improvements throughout the supply network. In the words of one participant: "If we can have greater transparency throughout the supply chain faster, we can begin to identify processes that need improving – such as in case of responding to food safety issues."

The prospect of realizing all of those benefits is the good news of blockchain. But that type of exposure comes with risks and requires vulnerability that's not always comfortable, easy or, at times, good for businesses. There are questions around issues such as security, confidentiality, liability, protecting proprietary information, regulatory compliance, integration with existing and evolving technologies, interoperability, the scarcity of technology talent, and agreements on standards.

That's partly why progress has been slow when it comes to proven, meaningful uses for blockchain. Matt Higginson, Marie-Claude Nadeau and Kausik Rajgopal pointed out in an article for McKinsey & Company that most blockchain prototypes in business are stuck in the pioneering phase of its lifecycle. "The bottom line," they wrote, "is that despite billions of dollars of investment, and nearly as many headlines, evidence for a practical scalable use for blockchain is thin on the ground" (Higginson *et al*, 2019). While blockchain advocates like Yiannas say "I haven't heard any challenges that I think are a show-stopper", they are realistic enough to understand that challenges exist and must be addressed if blockchain is to see the widespread adoption it needs to have the impact they predict. And, of course, that's part of the value of this book – it will help you navigate these challenges and better determine if, when and how blockchain might fit within your particular industry and for your particular company. We'll cover the dos and don'ts based on successful and failed pilots that will help you avoid getting stuck along the way.

Chain links: Key points from this chapter

- If blockchain lives up to its hype, many other supply chain technologies figure to grow in significance.

- Blockchain eventually will impact the way leaders, managers and consumers interact with and manage supply chains. But the hype of blockchain – even more so than the technology itself – is already radically influencing the future of supply chain management across the globe.

- You can do almost everything blockchain offers to the supply chain world by using existing database technologies. But you are not doing it. Therefore, the biggest reason blockchain matters to supply chain professionals is because the hype around the technology is causing an inescapable sea change across all facets of supply networks. It is pushing and pulling the supply chain world towards innovations it should have implemented over the past 20 years.

- Adding blockchain to broken processes and systems won't fix the broken processes and systems. All that gives you is broken processes and systems that are automated.

- Entering flawed data into a blockchain platform won't sanitize the data. The stinky garbage you put in will stink just as much when it comes out.

- The hype around blockchain's potential applications to the supply chain has spiked, but has been holding steady even without any applications that have demonstrated widespread, scalable success. So, the hype is outrunning its proven success stories, causing it to defy the pattern represented in the traditional hype cycle.

References

Agar, J (2013) *Constant Touch: A global history of the mobile phone*, Icon Books, London

Feinstein, S (2018) Blockchain: Catalyst for Disruptive Thinking [Blog], *RevUnit*, 31 May. http://blog.revunit.com/blockchain-catalyst-disruptive-thinking/ (archived at perma.cc/J6J4-NT5X)

Gartner (2019) Hype cycle methodology, *Gartner*. www.gartner.com/en/research/methodologies/gartner-hype-cycle (archived at perma.cc/LX2Y-D52Q)

Higginson, M, Nadeau, M and Rajgopal, K (2019) Blockchain's Occam Problem, *McKinsey & Company*, January. www.mckinsey.com/industries/financial-services/our-insights/blockchains-occam-problem (archived at perma.cc/9QVZ-RHD2)

Keller, J (2018) Interview with the authors for this book, 14 June

Kshertri, N (2018) Blockchain's role in meeting key supply chain management objectives, *International Journal of Information Management*, **39**, pp 80–9

Lovelock, J *et al* (2017) Forecast: Blockchain Business Value, Worldwide, 2017–2030, Gartner, 2 March. www.gartner.com/doc/3627117/forecast-blockchain-business-value-worldwide (archived at perma.cc/M5FW-SWHQ)

Olson, P (2019) This Reclusive Engineer Is Plotting the Death of Blockchain, *Forbes.com*, 9 January. www.forbes.com/sites/parmyolson/2019/01/09/this-hermitic-engineer-is-plotting-the-death-of-blockchain/ (archived at perma.cc/2D2K-KML7)#1b4ea7b5378e

Steelman, Z (2018) Interview with the authors for this book, 2 February

Von Clausewitz, K (2016) Winner Take All, *Time*, 16 September www.cnn.com/ALLPOLITICS/1996/analysis/time/9609/16/main.shtml (archived at perma.cc/5J3E-DNFH)

World Economic Forum (2015) Deep Shift: Technology Tipping Points and Societal Impact, September. www3.weforum.org/docs/WEF_GAC15_Technological_Tipping_Points_report_2015.pdf (archived at perma.cc/VVT4-D5LL)

Yiannas, F (2017) Interview with the authors for this book, 22 December

Walker, M (2018) Hype cycle for emerging technologies, Gartner, 6 August

Barriers to adopting blockchain

04

Johannes Gutenberg, the late German goldsmith-turned-inventor, developed a new-fangled contraption nearly six hundred years ago that could mass-produce hype in ways the world had never seen. Ironically, there was very little actual hype surrounding his invention of the printing press. If there had been, however, there certainly would have been critics and sceptics.

Change the world? they might have scoffed. Certainly not for the better! This thing, if it ever catches on, will be the end of civilized society. It will put information in the hands and minds of those who have no use for it and no understanding of it. And just think how quickly it will allow false information to spread. Besides, what's the rush? Do we really need to print 250 pages in an hour? Better to leave the work of the scribes to the scribes!

Back then, Gutenberg's printing press was, in our modern terms, a beta technology. Unproven, unstable, immature – in other words, it was right where we find blockchain today. Many firms don't easily tolerate beta projects. They have no appetite for projects that lack a definite scope or budget and that inevitably reveal new challenges for implementation.

It didn't take long for Gutenberg's invention to overcome the resistance – of which there was some, but not much – and to truly begin to change the world. But "didn't take long" is relative. Gutenberg began working on his printing press around 1436. The first known official record of this monumental invention, however, didn't occur until 1439, when witnesses in a lawsuit against Gutenberg described it in their testimony. Gutenberg eventually opened a printing shop in

Mainz, Germany, and it was there that he printed a copy of the Bible in Latin at some point between 1452 and 1454 – nearly 20 years after creating his invention.

By 1481 (another 30 years), it's been estimated that there were printing shops in at least 40 German cities, as many as 40 in Italy, and more than 20 in the Netherlands. Adoption outside of Europe, however, took even more time. Colonists, merchants and missionaries made use of the printing press as they moved around newly discovered parts of the world, but some local cultures resisted. This type of printing, for instance, was banned in the Ottoman Empire from 1483 to 1729 due to opposition from Muslim scribes and scholars.

The technology, of course, eventually was adopted widely around the world, opening the way for mass communication that has changed every aspect of society. It allowed Martin Luther to famously nail a copy of his Ninety-five Theses to the door of the All Saints' Church in Wittenberg, Germany, sparking the Reformation, and it was instrumental in spreading ideas and inspiring people behind the cause of democracy in what would become the United States of America. Historian David Ramsey argued that "the pen and press had merit equal to that of the sword" in the battle for independence.

The printing press created a literate audience and a means of reaching it, which drove further innovations and adoptions, eventually resulting in digital communications that now give print a novelty feel.

Nearly 550 years passed between the invention of the printing press and the invention of the internet. The adoption of those technologies occurred at vastly different speeds, but they share common themes. How long will it take for blockchain adoption? It's impossible to know, of course, but Brian Behlendorf, Executive Director of Hyperledger, said in 2016 that it's "still in the early stages of a 20-year, if not 50-year, adoption and maturation cycle" (Behlendorf, 2016). In other words, a long time.

Identifying hurdles

An enterprise architect and digital manager for a global fast-moving consumer goods (FMCG) company based in Europe summed up something we consistently heard from blockchain technologists. "It's not about the technology," he told us. "The technology is not so hard. It's about understanding process and getting partners" (Anonymous, 2018).

We asked the alumni of our executive MBA programme who attended our blockchain workshop about the most common barriers to implementation they have faced, and issues around a "lack of understanding" topped their list (Figure 4.1).

Among other things, the participants raised questions and recognized a need to develop a greater understanding of how to integrate blockchain into their supply chain process, the benefits, the costs and the ROI. In the words of one participant: "It is not hard or expensive to start a blockchain pilot. But beyond the initial technical proof of concept and the initial pilot, the question becomes how to scale throughout the supply chain and what will the cost and the ROI of that be – we don't know enough about that yet."

It was clear from the discussions during the workshop that the concerns were far less about the technology and a lot more about how to adopt and roll the technology out well. This implies that managers have made progress when it comes to use-case development and technological approaches. This is positive because research indicates that the technology is sometimes picked first and the problem is applied to a blockchain solution afterwards (Verhoeven *et al*, 2018).

Summarizing the barriers

We'll talk about creating the processes and partnerships in later chapters on implementation. When we get there, however, it will be helpful to have a foundational understanding of the most significant barriers to blockchain adoption.

After evaluating the various research, interviews and literature, we can conclude that leaders should focus most on nine significant barriers to adoption of blockchain within supply chains. Not surprisingly, most of them fit under the broad category of navigating the partnerships.

Figure 4.1   Barriers to implementation

Barrier	Value
LOU about integrating blockchain into existing process	4.05
LOU about potential benefits	4.00
LOU of costs and ROI	4.00
Uncertainty about ROI	3.89
LOU about technical limitations of blockchain	3.80
Lack of business case for blockchain	3.70
Lack of understanding (LOU) about blockchain technology	3.70
Cost of blockchain implementation	3.55
Privacy concerns	3.50
Integration issues with existing technologies	3.45
Security concerns about data integrity	3.40
Limited scalability of blockchain applications	3.39
Cost of blockchain	3.32
LOU about security/regulatory issues	3.30
Lack of speed of the blockchain	3.30
Lack of inter-operability of blockchain applications	3.26
Lack of data quality/integrity	3.21
Training needs	3.20
Large number of stakeholders involved in the decision making	3.16
Cost of blockchain pilots	3.16
Administrative burden on upstream supply chain partners	3.16
Lack of standards	3.05
Difficulty analysing information on the blockchain	3.05
Database integration difficulties	3.00
Lack of data security of blockchain	2.89
Lack of data integrity of blockchain	2.89
Usage difficulties for employees	2.80
Technical issues with hardware and software for blockchain	2.75
System reliability issues	2.70

Collaboration

All of the players within a supply network must contribute to the blockchain because blockchain is a team sport. Any significant participant in the supply chain who can't or won't participate represents, at best, an inefficiency in the process and, at worst, a roadblock to success.

Ramesh Gopinath, Vice President of Blockchain Solutions at IBM, told Louise Matsakis of Wired.com that convincing everyone in the supply chain to switch to blockchain is one of the biggest hurdles when it comes to using the technology in supply networks. "You've got to make sure that everybody in the ecosystem gets something out of it," Gopinath said. "That is very hard and it takes a long time to figure out" (Matsakis, 2018).

Potential players typically don't participate because they don't see the benefits to their organization, they fear that participating will provide too many benefits to their competition, their business lacks financial stability, they are generally resistant to process and technology changes, they have security concerns, or some combination of all of those things.

Some organizations, especially those in a traditional middleman role, as well as some individuals within organizations, may resist (passively or actively) out of fear of losing their jobs to the new technology. This is a common challenge for gaining buy-in with most new technology, and it has been evident, for instance, as a barrier for RFID adoption.

Frank Yiannas told us that one of Walmart's role as a pioneer of blockchain is to sell the benefits to potential partners and make it easier for them to get on board. "We genuinely believe that it's a data model that allows for the creation of shared value," he said. "That's an important concept for us – shared value. With blockchain, everybody can obtain value out of the ecosystem and the value that you've shared" (Yiannas, 2017).

One of the big values of blockchain in food safety, he found, is that it not only quickly identifies the source of a problem, but it also quickly exonerates the players who had no part in the problem. Farmers and processors loved that idea, he said, because it saves their reputation. This is important during a food safety crisis, of course, but also in more ordinary situations. The processing plant, for instance, is often blamed when a product has a shorter than expected shelf life, but blockchain helps them prove they moved it efficiently through their part of the ecosystem. Blockchain also allows farmers to connect with customers in ways like never before, because customers can scan a package of lettuce and learn, in great detail, about the farmer who grew it. "So, this concept of shared value is why people will participate in a blockchain ecosystem," Yiannas said. "It's more democratized" (Yiannas, 2017).

Standardization

Finding willing participants, however, is just one hurdle. Each player also needs to participate with agreed-upon standards and definitions or else, like any other shared database, it doesn't work efficiently and might not work at all.

GS1, of course, is in the business of developing standards, so it's no surprise that it's involved in the blockchain discussion. Gena Morgan, a consultant with GS1 US, points out that "transactions written to a shared ledger require standardization. Unique identity and a standard language are core to supply chain visibility. Otherwise, who knows what anybody's saying?"

Yiannas, who supports following the lead of GS1 on standards, sees blockchain as a catalyst for more widespread adoption of standards because standards are essential to success with blockchains. "If you try to do it without it," he said, "you find yourself maybe not as bad but very similar to where you are today, which is systems that don't speak to each other. ... Standards are the DNA to build the system" (Yiannas, 2017).

Standards, which were also an issue with the adoption of supply chain technologies like RFID and EDI, come in all shapes and sizes. They might look like the barcodes on a product, but they also include the jargon of a company or an industry. When IBM worked with Kansas City Southern Railway, for instance, the pilot required that data from the cargo shipping company match the data used by the railroad industry. At first, however, the programmers found nothing in the shipping documents that referenced the weight of the containers, which is a key piece in the railroad's data puzzle. After some discussions with the shipping partners, they realized the weight could be calculated based on information identified by a three-letter acronym on each container. TEU, which stands for "20-foot-equivalent unit", measures a ship's capacity to carry cargo based on the volume of a standard 20-foot-long container. A TEU isn't a measure of mass; it provides enough information to draw conclusions.

Jeffrey Keller, a lead account partner with IBM, said once they figured that out, the problem was a "two-minute fix". But those kinds of details, he said, are critical in business-to-business communication. "That's one small example of why communication between multiple entities could be so complicated" (Keller, 2018).

And the more complex the environment, with multiple partners from multiple industries and multiple countries, the bigger the challenge. "This goes back, I think, to a fundamental challenge of EDI, where you could have different interpretations of the same word," Keller told us. "As much as we wanted a standard to exist within the EDI world, it only got so far. But these kinds of discussions… it's not rocket science, it's just taking one step at a time to get folks to speak a consistent language and have the appropriate translation in place so that information can flow more easily" (Keller, 2018).

Aligning on definitions and standards often works easily enough with a very linear supply chain, but even those have challenges. Dennis Gerson, also with IBM, recalled working with an FMCG company that had several different definitions of a "case" of product. In other words, depending upon the division within the company, a case might involve 2-litre bottles of carbonated beverages, 7-ounce juice boxes, or quart jars of pasta sauce.

"A case isn't a case isn't a case," Gerson told us. "Yes, they're using standards like GS1, but that just gives you the data format. It doesn't tell you what the definition of an item is. If you're doing intercompany supply chain in retail, you need to understand the definition of an item and the definition of an SKU. I mean, those basics don't go away with blockchain. If anything, those basics become more important, because once you put everything on the ledger and it's visible to the parties involved, they see the same information. Everyone's internal gobbledygook, internal mess, internal sausage becomes visible to their trading partners" (Gerson, 2018).

Standards are being addressed in several different ways. Programmers, for instance, are incorporating existing technologies (such as EDI) and using those standards when they do so. Walmart generally supports following the lead of GS1 on standards. Industry consortiums like BiTA are also working to create standards, although the processes of getting consensus from so many different players hasn't been quick and doesn't always solve the specific needs of every player. Industry alliances also need to factor in the reality that supply chains often interact between multiple industries. So, what happens when participants in a blockchain come from different industries that use different standards? In short, nothing much happens, because it doesn't work very well. Thus, while industry groups have a role to play on standards, they also need to work within the larger ecosystem.

Interoperability

One reason standards are vital is that blockchain partners need to work with compatible software. Right now, there are multiple versions. There's no off-the-shelf enterprise solution that a company can buy and immediately implement with dozens of partners. And there are multiple players competing to become the standard. Some inevitably will become the Betamax of blockchain, while others will emerge as the VHS.

Mike Naatz, a senior vice president of Kansas City Southern Railway, told us he sees that "people want to play together and cooperate, because they understand that it's going to be necessary to the success of the blockchain. But at the same time, they're trying to protect the business interests. And so, it's going to be very interesting to see how that plays out over time" (Naatz, 2018).

It's one thing for blockchain to work well in a pilot that involves six or seven partners, but the larger the ecosystem, the more complicated it becomes. As companies move past the pilot stages and look to scale, they may find that additional key partners are ready to join in – but with some different type of blockchain that they've created with their own pilot programme.

Keller believes blockchain solutions that are done the right way will be capable of merging with other well-architected blockchains. But key to this happening, he said, is for players who compete in the marketplace to partner for their common good. That's why, for instance, you see IBM working with SAP. But smaller players – the entrepreneurs who are often nimbler and disruptively innovative – are less likely to work with the big players, either because they don't want to or because they aren't invited to the party.

Walmart's Cameron Geiger points out that some enterprise solutions providers build their solutions so that the user gets locked into their exclusive ecosystem. A proprietary solution can work in a simple supply chain or in a supply network that's highly controlled and closed. For instance, a vertical manufacturer could create a proprietary blockchain application that would track parts right down to the batch in which they were produced. The same concept can be expanded to third-party original equipment manufacturers (OEMs), where finished manufacturing and assembly is limited to a few competitors who agree to use the same system or platform. But this would work because it's a closed supply chain network.

More complex supply networks with multiple participants who buy and sell from multiple participants need greater flexibility. For instance, let's say you are a farmer who grows rice, soybeans and cotton. Any or all of those crops might be sold to more than one distributor, so you'll want a blockchain platform that's cost- and time-effective. If different customers are on different proprietary platforms, you might opt out. You don't want to pay for more than one platform and you don't want to have to learn the ins and outs of more than one system. What you need is a customized solution that plays well with all the partners to your business, and that will likely only come from a platform using open-source software.

Bureaucracies

Most supply chains are now global ecosystems, which means that raw materials and materials often cross borders en route to their final destinations. While this represents one of the biggest opportunities for using blockchain to drive efficiencies, it also represents one of the bigger hurdles. Governments provide necessary checks and balances, oversight and regulation for commerce, but they often move like an ocean liner in the Panama Canal – they don't quickly or easily change direction.

Some governments and their various agencies are eager to explore the potential of blockchain, but getting them to approve and/or contribute data has been one of the bigger challenges for several pilots. Some are interested in playing a role but have yet to take part. And some are downright resistant to the technology because they see the transparency of blockchain as a threat to their control. We know of at least one project that by most measures was considered successful but that wasn't pursued beyond the pilot because the communist government didn't want the public exposure it might bring.

Competitive instincts

Competition between major links in the supply chain also presents a potential barrier. Major retailers, shippers, railways, trucking companies, distributors and manufacturers all have one thing in common – they want to find or maintain their hold on competitive advantages for their business. This can limit their desire to play well with others when turf wars emerge. "My hope is that the potential value of driving out efficiencies will counterbalance that competitive desire," Keller told us (Keller, 2018).

One area where participants must overcome this barrier to collaboration is around governance. A strength of blockchain is its decentralized nature, but business-to-business blockchains require agreements about things like who will write the code and who can see, use, share and analyse the data.

To highlight this dilemma, which you might notice is tightly connected to the previous challenges, consider the collaboration between Maersk and IBM on a blockchain solution for shipping. Maersk has invested heavily in creating a platform that can be used not only in its industry, but as a base platform for related industries like railroads, trucking and even manufacturers. This raised regulatory concerns from governments, and the eyebrows of Maersk's competitors in the shipping business.

Rolf Habben Jansen, CEO of Maersk rival Hapag-Lloyd, said the best platform will fail if it's "just a platform for Maersk and IBM". And with several other similar projects under development at the same time, it's hard to know which will emerge as something truly useful to the industry. "Without a joint solution," Habben told the 2018 Global Liner Shipping Conference, "we're going to waste a lot of money, and that would benefit no one" (Anderson and Vogdrup-Schmidt, 2018).

One promise of blockchain, of course, is that it provides an equal footing for all the players who use it. The reality is that companies may have to sacrifice some of their current competitive advantage to reap greater rewards in other areas. Some parts of supply chain efficiency, for instance, might become more of a level playing field, while things like customer service, quality, or the ability to create and use data insights will grow in importance.

The governance also has to be structured in ways that ensure trust between parties that can be partners and competitors at the same time. Take retail as an example. Competing vendors all might want and need to be on the same blockchain with various major retailers, but they all will want assurances that their competitors can't access trade secrets and that the retailers can't access information that gives them an unfair advantage when negotiating price. Most blockchain architects we spoke to believe this is easily solved with permissioned-based blockchains, but they still need to prove it over time in pilots that evolve into implemented systems.

"Blockchain networks must clearly establish rules for self-governance, including membership, data ownership, rules of conduct, and privacy," Yiannas wrote in a 2018 article for the MIT journal *Innovations*. "Blockchain is about trust" (Yiannas, 2018). This, he said, is why Walmart reached out to competitors like Kroger and Wegmans and suppliers like Tyson and Nestlé to become founding partners of a blockchain alliance. "It was… important to ensure that the self-governance structure we built around the blockchain network to resolve issues such as data ownership, privacy, and access rights was done collaboratively with the Foundation Partners," he said, "in order to prevent any one stakeholder, like Walmart or our solution provider IBM, unequal authority to make decisions" (Yiannas, 2018).

Immutability

Another challenge for blockchain is the dark side of immutability. One of the big promises of blockchain technology is the idea that entries into this type of shared and encrypted database can't be changed. The data, therefore, are more reliable and permanently visible to the players who need to see them. But there is a reason why most existing data technologies follow the CRUD model – they allow users to Create, Read, Update and Delete data.

"In the world of blockchain," Keller points out, "there's no update and no delete. You only create and then offer the opportunity to read data. And because of that, an architect will advise, rightfully so, to keep the amount of data you actually write into the blockchain highly architected and very disciplined" (Keller, 2018).

In a perfect world, "highly architected and very disciplined" means fewer garbage data enter the system, but it could also mean that some valuable data are inadvertently left out. It also means that there's no way to clean up or delete garbage data that find their way in. And even great data have a shelf life. Many businesses are accustomed to destroying records as soon as they are legally allowed to do so, but a truly immutable system means that records never go away.

At best, the participants in the blockchain can, by consensus, agree to destroy the access code that allows visibility to certain data. The data don't go away, but they can no longer be seen. It's sort of like the tree that falls in the woods when no one is around – it makes a sound, but no one hears it. This solution only works if everyone – including regulators – agrees to it on the front end and the system is designed to make it happen.

Security

Before investing in blockchain technology, responsible business leaders understandably want a high level of confidence that the platform really provides a stable and secure system that's not vulnerable to cyberattacks by hackers, falsified information by self-serving parties, or network outages from human-caused or natural disasters.

Proponents of blockchains are quick to point out the inherent security of the technology. Blockchains themselves have never been hacked, they say. John Monarch, the CEO of ShipChain, echoed the comments of other blockchain advocates we interviewed when he told us that: "Any issues have been with private companies who have made new software for it. But there's never been a crack in any of the systems." But that doesn't make blockchains 100 per cent reliable.

Blockgeeks.com, a site that creates training around blockchain technology, points out that its "decentralized applications aren't faultless". The code written into smart contracts and other applications, after all, is written by fallible human beings.

"Smart contracts are only as good as the people who write them," the site points out. "Code bugs or oversights can lead to unintended adverse actions being taken. If a mistake in the code gets exploited, there is no efficient way in which an attack or exploitation can be stopped other than obtaining a network consensus and rewriting the underlying code. This goes against the essence of the blockchain which is meant to be immutable. Also, any action taken by a central party raises serious questions about the decentralized nature of an application" (BlockGeeks, 2017).

Cody Hopkins, an early adopter of blockchain in his role as General Manager of Grass Roots Farmers' Cooperative, also points out that the "technology does not prevent lying. It just doesn't". In other words, a manager could upload false information about quality control standards into a blockchain and, without enough checks and balances, create an immutable but totally false record.

But Hopkins and others contend that blockchains discourage such dishonesty. The manager who is tempted to upload false information knows that the information is encrypted forever and connected to him or her with a unique digital signature. And he or she knows that any fudged numbers in the maths will likely be exposed by the system's computations.

"People can lie," Hopkins said, "but there are documented transactions that are going on. If we say we bought a batch of chickens from this farm and upload the invoice as documentation, both parties have to agree to it" (Hopkins, 2017).

And that agreement is digitally saved on the blockchain forever. "Right now, if you get something that's antibiotic-free, there's essentially an affidavit that somebody has signed," Hopkins said. "You're dealing with a document that someone could tamper with or lose.

The blockchain is so much more advanced than that. In our case, you have a transfer of assets that's captured in an immutable, distributed ledger. You have documentation uploaded to support that. That's so much better than an affidavit on paper' (Hopkins, 2017).

In some cases, blockchains not only discourage dishonesty but also reward honesty. Some incentives are tangible, like rewards in cryptocurrency that can be exchanged to purchase things, while other rewards are less concrete, like appealing to the group's shared reputation.

"Blockchain prevents someone tampering with the information," Hopkins said. "And there's this incentive piece that's built into these networks. We're just scratching the surface. But you've got this eco-system of individual entities and all their reputations are tied together. It helps build trust over time" (Hopkins, 2017).

Garbage in

Blockchain isn't a saviour for failing processes and bad information. If you are trying to automate broken processes, you'll end up with automated but still broken processes. If you use blockchain to clean up bad data, you just end up with bad data on a blockchain.

One of the promises of EDI was better data. While it moved things forward in that regard, EDI didn't enforce the type of discipline between partners that would assure clean, reliable data. "I think in the world of blockchain," Keller told us, "what we're going to see is that the participants who begin to win are those who are going to make sure the data that is put in the blockchain is accurate because that's what's going to be trusted" (Keller, 2018).

Organizations that simply find another way to automate the status quo will only add noise and confusion to their supply networks. The winners will look for processes with improvement opportunities and see if blockchain adds value that makes those processes better.

Cost

And then there's the cost and ROI associated with blockchain, which, to some degree, remain relatively unknown. Cost is a common barrier for most new technologies. With RFID, for instance, it was the cost of tags and readers, as well as the uneven ROI among the various parties. For some, the ROI was significant and justified the expense, but retailers tended to experience more of the benefits while manufacturers felt overly burdened by an expense that mainly provided efficiencies to other players in the supply chain.

While blockchain promises a more shared ROI and can create some cost-saving efficiencies, it also will create new costs for software and IT experts who understand it at a more granular level. The cost of testing a blockchain use case is relatively low compared to technologies like RFID that included an investment in equipment. The initial cost of a pilot is largely found in the time invested by the team that plans and implements it.

As IBM's Gerson told us, when executives realize they're going to need "six pretty darn smart people for eight to twelve weeks... working on this 25 per cent of the time", that's a barrier for some companies. "They go, 'Well, maybe we'll want to do a little bit more education first'" (Gerson, 2018).

There's also a cost for storing all the data. The bigger, more complex a blockchain network grows, the more data it stores and the more power it consumes for computing consensus and the more storage is required to hold the data. The efficiencies may offset the new cost, but that ROI remains to be proven.

"People talk about, 'Oh, it's cheap,'" said Keller, "but the reality is there's some costly dimensions to the underlying technology" (Keller, 2018). Driving those costs down – or completely out – is a role many of the pioneers believe they must play to reduce the barriers and drive widespread adoption that benefits everyone.

"We have to deliver a blockchain world where the cost of participation is zero," Yiannas told us. "Similar to social media networks where people get into the networks but there's no pain point or barrier that prevents them from getting in. And then the more value you extract from that network, there might be a transaction fee or a cost" (Yiannas, 2017).

The digital divide

What makes blockchain unique in the context of supply networks is that the supply chain, unlike with most other contexts that use blockchain, operates in both the physical and digital worlds. Most other uses for blockchain never leave the digital world. You can't roll a bitcoin around your fingers; it exists only in cyberspace, and that's just fine for those who use it.

Supply networks, meanwhile, move physical products through a physical world. While many elements of the process are handled electronically, the digital is almost always connected to a physical resource or product. And at some point, the shipment of a physical version of a pair of shoes must land on a physical version of someone's feet. Thus, leaders throughout supply networks need a blockchain that meshes its digital advantages with physical realities. They need an exact replica of the physical world that's available in digital form. Therein lies one of the biggest challenges, because the physical world is prone to error, intentional or accidental.

MIT professors Catherine Tucker and Christian Catalini used the example of "tracking babies" to illustrate this dilemma in an article for *Harvard Business Review*. Using blockchain to store immutable and verifiable records containing a baby's location seems like an awesome idea, but it comes with a big challenge: "How does someone know which digital record is attached to which baby?"

For starters, the baby would need a tag, chip, genome record, or some other futuristic physical identifier that links to the baby's digital record. For babies, this would present moral and ethical issues. If you got beyond those, which would be the case with a chip for a physical product like the bumper for a pickup truck, there's a bigger problem: blockchain can't verify that the right physical marker was initially connected to the proper physical product. In other words, it still depends on a fallible human being to bridge the gap between the digital and physical worlds.

"In our example," wrote Tucker and Catalini, "the technology would have to rely on humans to correctly and honestly implement the match between baby and digital record. And if humans get that wrong or manipulate the data when it is entered, in a system where records are believed ex-post as having integrity, this can have serious negative consequences" (Tucker and Catalina, 2018).

Blockchain advocates believe that incentives and cross-checks between partners can prevent errant or manipulated records, but clearly the stakes are high when it's put in human terms. And while an incorrect or manipulated data about turnip greens obviously isn't as appalling as errors in medical records, it still can have huge negative consequences, both to the health and well-being of consumers and to the bottom line of the business.

Burgers and barriers

Some of these barriers may be lessened as complementary technologies, especially IoT, become more accessible. McDonald's, for example, has been testing a "Freshness and Expiration Management" pilot with hamburgers that integrates blockchain with IoT. When there's a malfunction with a truck hauling refrigerated meats and the temperature in the container (or reefer) drops, the expiration date on the product must be adjusted to an earlier date. In most of the current food delivery processes, the transportation carrier's data logger easily could change the data without the shipper knowing the temperature had gone up.

Here is where combination of blockchain and IoT comes into play. In the McDonald's pilot, RFID readers (IoT) are placed on every box in the reefer, which sends information to the blockchain. This allows McDonald's to ensure the data are accurate and to know when and where the temperature changed.

The transportation carrier's data logger still could tamper with the RFID readers and adjust the temperatures that are sent to the blockchain, but that data logger would need to have expert technical skills to pull this off. So, this scenario is far less likely than the scenario without blockchain.

Blockchain becomes much more powerful for supply chains when combined with IoT, analytics, machine learning and AI. For one example, the McDonald's Freshness and Expiration Management pilot is providing value well beyond lowering the risk that data loggers might manipulate temperature data. By adding analytics to the IoT-enabled blockchain, McDonald's is able to improve the freshness of hamburgers delivered to their restaurants. After their beef is grinded, blended, formed into patties, and packaged and sealed into cases, RFID labels are placed on the cases. The label is encoded and scanned to the blockchain. These data inform freshness information by setting the expiration date.

The RFID tag is scanned again when the case enters and exits the storage cooler (in the same production facility), and the RFID is also scanned when the case exits the production facility. The case is also scanned at entry and exit in the transportation and the distribution centre activities as it flows through the supply chain to the restaurant. Finally, the restaurant scans the case when it arrives and is placed into the cooler.

At each point, the RFID tag is connected to temperature sensors, which communicate data to the blockchain. If the temperature drops below specifications at any point along this food chain, analytics of the temperature and associated product life characteristics may 1) adjust the expiration date (if the temperature dropped below a certain specified point) or 2) determine that the case is spoiled and should not be used. The restaurant employee then scans the RFID and, based on analytics of the temperatures throughout the food chain and associated product life characteristics, learns which case should be pulled from the cooler next based on the case that is closest to expiration.

Other existing technologies also are being used within blockchain projects. Data already collected through EDI, for instance, can be uploaded into the blockchain – so long as the data are good and the standard consistent.

Unanswered questions

Ultimately, every existing option still comes with limitations, questions that can't be answered, or both. They all require technical assistance to set up and run, and every competing entity brings its own jargon – the insider words and phrases that make the system simple and understandable to them but that often confuse the hell out of everyone else. And, by the way, the investment isn't small, and the payoffs aren't always clear or guaranteed.

So where does that leave supply chain practitioners? Well, there's no single answer that fits for everyone other than this: don't wait to start figuring it out.

For many supply chain leaders, the critical question about any new technology boils down to this: How will it help create a more efficient and effective process? The idea of a truly transparent supply chain isn't quite as threatening if, for instance, it will help with forecasting and inventory management. Operations-minded managers want answers to some legitimate and practical questions: To what degree can it reduce the bullwhip effect? How will it enable smart contracts that lead to more efficient sourcing and purchasing? Will blockchain reduce costs? Will it add value to the overall supply chain system?

So, before we take a deep dive into the process for developing, evaluating and implementing a test case for using blockchain, let's look at the specific ways the technology could impact key components of modern supply networks.

Chain links: Key points from this chapter

- The biggest barriers to blockchain adoption are: collaboration, standardization, interoperability, bureaucracies, competitive instincts, immutability, security, garbage in, and cost.

- Blockchain is unique in the context of supply networks because, unlike with most other contexts that use blockchain, it must operate in both the physical and digital worlds.

- Blockchain becomes much more powerful for supply chains and adoption will come much more quickly when it is combined with technologies such as IoT, analytics, machine learning and AI.

References

Anderson, O and Vogdrup-Schmidt, L (2018) Rivals Reject Blockchain Solution from Maersk and IBM, *ShippingWatch*, 15 May. https://shippingwatch.com/carriers/Container/article10602520.ece (archived at perma.cc/9LDD-GELR)

Anonymous (2018) Interview with the authors for this book, 8 June

Behlendorf, B (2016) Meet Hyperledger: An 'Umbrella' for Open Source Blockchain & Smart Contract Technologies [Blog], *Hyperledger*, 13 September. hyperledger.org/blog/2016/09/13/meet-hyperledger-an-umbrella-for-open-source-blockchain-smart-contract-technologies (archived at perma.cc/5TPC-4SKP)

BlockGeeks (2017) What is Ethereum? The Most Comprehensive Guide Ever!, *BlockGeeks*. https://blockgeeks.com/guides/what-is-ethereum/ (archived at perma.cc/YP6Q-3ZHL)

Gerson, D (2018) Interview with the authors for this book, 6 August

Hopkins, C (2017) Interview with the authors for this book, 9 November

Keller, J (2018) Interview with the authors for this book, 14 June

Matsakis, L (2018) Following a Tuna from Fiji to Brooklyn – on the Blockchain, *Wired*, 22 May. https://www.wired.com/story/following-a-tuna-from-fiji-to-brooklynon-the-blockchain/ (archived at perma.cc/AJ2F-S3T9)

Naatz, M (2018) Interview with the authors for this book, 1 June

Tucker, C and Catalina, C (2018) What Blockchain Can't Do, *Harvard Business Review*, 28 June. https://hbr.org/2018/06/what-blockchain-cant-do (archived at perma.cc/3AZR-ETHV)

Verhoeven, P, Sinn, F and Herden, TT (2018) Examples for blockchain implementations in logistics and supply chain management: exploring the mindful use of a new technology, *Logistics*, **2** (20)

Yiannas, F (2017) Interview with the authors for this book, 22 December

Yiannas, F (2018) A new era of food transparency powered by blockchain, *Innovations: Technology, Governance, Globalization*, **12** (1–2), pp 46–56 [Also Online] https://www.mitpressjournals.org/doi/abs/10.1162/inov_a_00266 (archived at perma.cc/35TF-WTM2)

PART TWO
Supply ecosystems

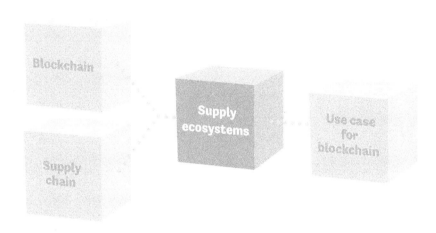

Networking supply chains

We noted earlier that blockchain isn't your grandparents' ledger. And it's a good thing, too, because we don't work in a world that operates with your grandparents' supply chain systems. Or even your parents' supply chain systems, for that matter. Indeed, two seismic transformations are sweeping through global supply chains, and both figure to reshape the landscape in ways that not only need but will demand solutions like blockchain technology.

First, supply chains are becoming **increasingly complex**. They no longer resemble the traditional chains that once linked manufacturers and suppliers. Supply chains now consist of a vast array of different and interconnected parts. Second, supply chains and operations are getting **increasingly dynamic**. The systems, environments, relationships and interactions not only are more complex, but they also are constantly moving and changing.

The increased complexity has turned many supply chains into massive networked ecosystems with multiple products moved through and by multiple parties that are all trying to work together. It's not uncommon for a single company to have contracts with multiple manufacturers, all drawing upon a similar supplier network and feeding a range of distribution models, from traditional retail stores to online consignment services. Gone are the days of Ford's famous River Rouge plant that was renowned for taking raw iron ore, glass and rubber in on one side and rolling vehicles out of the other side. Today, most companies buy complex, pre-assembled parts from a wide network of suppliers. Some outsource their entire manufacturing operations. Cisco, Microsoft and Apple do not have any manufacturing facilities of their own – they only handle the design, marketing, sales and supply chain.

Products have become much more complex, as well. A car, for instance, may have 50,000 parts. A bill of materials (BOM), which lists the quantities of subassemblies, parts and raw materials required to make one unit of a product, can go on for page after page after page. The BOM for an automobile, for example, would include one body, one engine, one transmission, four door assemblies, two axles, four brake assemblies, four-wheel assemblies, a navigation system, and so on. The assembled engine might include an engine block, six pistons, six fuel injectors, six spark plugs, twelve valves and so on. And companies with multiple products will have a different BOM for each product.

With product complexity comes the need to use more suppliers, who, in turn, may use more suppliers, which adds even more complexity to supply chains. A car seat, for instance, used to be like a piece of furniture and depended only on suppliers of cloth, leather, stuffing and framing. Modern car seats include switches, motors, heaters, sensors and microprocessors.

Today's supply chains can also be quite deep. Intel sources tantalum, a metal essential to its microprocessors, through as many as a dozen supply chain steps that go back through the makers of electronic components that contain tantalum to the metal processors, smelters, ore exporters, transporters, all the way to the artisanal miners.

The increasing complexity would be easier to manage if it were more static, but that's clearly not the case. Just the opposite, in fact. Today's reality may or may not be true tomorrow or next week, which is why this increasingly dynamic reality is the second major transformation that's affecting supply chains.

A large supply network may have an overwhelming number of interactions and interdependencies among different firms, processes and resources. Supply networks have a wide geographic distribution. Customers can initiate transactions at any time with little or no regard for existing load, thus contributing to a noisy network character. It is increasingly harder to separate signal from noise.

The many moving parts of the modern supply chains include:

- the parts that go into the company's products;
- the identities of suppliers who make these parts;
- the locations where these parts are made, assembled and distributed;
- the flows of parts and products, including the transportation links that move materials along the chain;
- the inventories of materials, parts and finished goods that are stored or being handled in various stages of the chain.

The expanding mosaic of supply networks poses unprecedented risks for supply chain leaders. Big companies, for example, may have no contact with or may even be unaware of some lower-tier suppliers. A disruption in the operations of these suppliers can have a surprisingly huge impact on the big firm. An explosion in 2012 at a German factory owned by Evonik Industries, for instance, wreaked havoc in the car industry. That's because the factory supplied 70 per cent of the world's demand for a particular type of nylon resin used to make brake and fuel lines. Weather (hurricanes, tornados, volcanic eruptions, wildfires, floods, droughts, snowstorms), political unrest, labour disputes, and bankruptcies are among the other uncontrollable factors that can have massive effects on supply networks.

The more complex and dynamic the networks, the greater the need to do at least five things that blockchain promises to provide:

1 Record the transactions between multiple parties in a secure and permanent way.

2 Make these records traceable and auditable.

3 Find ways to manage transactions that are dependent on many of the previous transactions involving multiple parties, all of whom need to enter or retrieve data.

4 Create a degree of trust between manufacturers and suppliers within the network who do not know each other.

5 Quickly establish the identity and provenance of many high-cost and/or mission-critical items.

The shifts from simple supply chains – links that connect each other – to supply networks within complex and dynamic ecosystems will make network theory an increasingly important component to supply chain management. So, network theory plays a key role in understanding and implementing blockchain solutions.

Network theory uses graphs to represent the symmetric and asymmetric relationships between disconnected objects. For blockchain, those objects are all the "nodes", or computers, that make up a given blockchain ecosystem. In the case of supply chain management, those "objects" could be every person within every organization that plays a role in moving a product from raw material to production to retail to the consumer.

Network theory allows us to provide a simple visual representation of the changing dynamics of supply chain systems. This allows us to make smarter use of the relationships and connections involved in the network.

To understand how network theory works (and applies to blockchain), let's start with a simple example of the flow of information from one vendor to a retailer. Then we can see how that expands to a more complex reality.

Figure 5.1   Retailer vendor

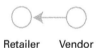

Retailer   Vendor

Now add a second tier – a supplier to the vendor.

Figure 5.2   Retailer vendor supplier

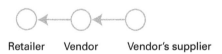

Retailer   Vendor   Vendor's supplier

Now toss in multiple vendors with their suppliers.

Figure 5.3   Retailer vendor multiple supplier

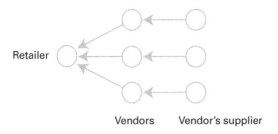

Retailer

Vendors   Vendor's supplier

Now consider that those vendors also supply each other and/or other retailers.

Figure 5.4   Supply chain ecosystem

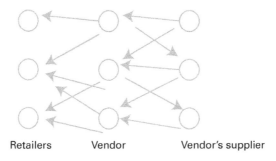

Retailers   Vendor   Vendor's supplier

As you can see, the ecosystems are interconnected and complex, which means blockchain figures to provide considerable value if it can provide visibility into those connections and insights that help leaders make more informed, strategic decisions.

Embedding new ideas

No two supply networks are exactly the same and all supply networks, as we noted earlier, are increasingly dynamic and complex. But network theory allows us to look at the dimensions common to all networks, examine how those dimensions impact supply networks in their three most common stages, and better understand the potential benefits of blockchain during each stage.

The two common dimensions of networks that are most relevant to our discussion about supply networks and blockchain are **structural** embeddedness and relational embeddedness. Those might sound pretty complicated, but that's only because they are terms created by academics (like us). We'll break them down one at a time, starting with structural embeddedness.

Stanford Professor Mark Granovetter was the first to start talking about what's now referred to as structural embeddedness. Three decades ago, he claimed that the choice of economic action and outcomes, like all social action and outcomes, is affected not only by the relationships of the people involved, but also by the structure of the overall network of relationships. Later research confirmed that such structural embeddedness was, in fact, responsible for a great deal of the order and the disorder within firms and entire industries.

Simply put, structural embeddedness involves how relationships are configured or structured. This is the impersonal side of the interactions. The structure, for instance, might determine your access to a supplier or buyer. The structure might allow you direct access to one or two key players, but not to people deeper within that organization or to the companies that supply that organization. There are two important things about structural embeddedness. First, you can't always control it. Second, there may be holes in it.

University of Chicago Professor Ronald Burt, who developed the concept of "structural holes", defines them as "a gap between two individuals with complementary resources or information". If you are part of a closely connected group, for instance, everyone in that group has access to each other, and information and resources are readily shared. If your access to another group is limited to one individual in that group, then your information and resources are limited to what that person shares with you. He or she acts as a filter, which means you may get less information than you need or you might not get some information as quickly as you need it.

This is extremely common in business relationships where a sale or account rep, for instance, might be the primary or only point of contact between her company and another company. Even though her company might have multiple teams that in some way work on the account, the flow of information is filtered through her.

The more you can close the gap in the structure that connects your two networks – in other words, create better access to other members in the other network – the better your information and resources and the greater likelihood that you can use your network connection as a competitive advantage.

In Figure 5.5, the only connection between two clusters of companies is between companies A and B. These two companies may belong to different industries. Company A might be a specialty fabric manufacturer, for instance, and company B might be a fashion apparel producer with a dense distribution network. Company A is B's supplier but B has virtually no knowledge about A's cluster of suppliers because A is the only link.

Figure 5.5   Structural hole between dense clusters

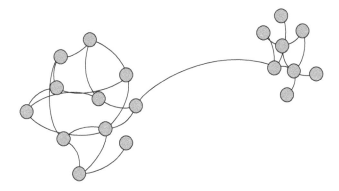

A and B also might be located in different countries. The lifeblood of any network is the flow of information, and structural holes slow down the flow. Geographic proximity helps increase the flow by increasing the likelihood that individuals will meet, interact, and explore common interests and shared beliefs. Physical proximity, however, is a luxury in today's far-flung supply networks. When a tsunami hit Japan in 2011, leading to a nuclear accident, many US companies that bought Japanese products or that moved goods through Japanese waters began to worry that their goods might be radioactive. Fear of radioactive foods, materials and dust created questions about the safety of everything coming from Japan.

Intel worried that radioactive dust might settle on or get into shipping containers passing through the area's ports, potentially affecting 7,000 of Intel's shipping lanes. Even if the chips that Intel sourced from Japan weren't radioactive themselves, exposure to radiation during manufacturing or transportation could have reduced their reliability. Intel had no means to ensure that chips and silicon weren't exposed to radiation at any stage. In a similar vein, Procter & Gamble worried about radioactive ingredients getting into the ingredients supplied by the Japanese chemical company BASF. These ingredients go into lipstick manufactured and sold by Procter & Gamble, so the company had to install Geiger counters on both the Japanese and Western sides of its supply chain.

Blockchain could come handy by creating visibility into such far-flung networks. A company could go from not knowing it is exposed to a disruption of a deep-tier supplier in a region that might be hit by a natural disaster, to knowing that it is exposed to such a risk, to even knowing that the supplier will be hit by a hurricane in three days but that this supplier has four weeks of inventory at a distribution centre in another, safer part of the country.

Blockchain, in other words, can reconfigure communication in global supply networks by providing virtual proximity to the structure of the relationships. This feeling of proximity is enabled by instantly distributing relevant and real-time data about processes and conditions that are likely to affect the company.

Many organizations already have attempted to create such proximity. Unilever, for example, has an internal organization, Ultra-Logistik, that is based in Poland and manages all Unilever transport movements in Europe. Centralizing all transportation procurement and operations (using Oracle's transport management system) yielded cost savings, reduced carbon footprint and increased visibility. And the Dutch Institute for Advanced Logistics developed "Cross Chain Control Centers" (4C) to coordinate and synchronize the flow of physical goods, information and finances of several worldwide supply chains relevant to the Netherlands. These systems are similar to airport control towers that choreograph the movements of aircraft on the ground and in the air. A central hub of technology, people and processes can capture and use supply chain data to enable short- and long-term decision making. Blockchain, on the other hand, does it in a decentralized way.

The virtual proximity allowed by blockchain provides two major benefits to information sharing: access and timing.

We all love access, right? If information is power, then access to information – accurate, relevant information – is critical to making good decisions and building solid insights for planning. Unfortunately, information usually isn't evenly spread across supply networks, because supply networks usually lack visibility, transparency and traceability. Some organizations are secretive. Some don't have the right technology. But one of the core reasons for the uneven spread of information is that companies are unevenly connected with one another. Companies mostly pay close attention to the information that's pertinent to them and their immediate partners. The flow of other types of information can easily overwhelm them. There are limits to the volume of information that organizations can process effectively. We can keep up with only so many books, articles, memos and news. Blockchain, however, may enable the network to become an important screening device. With blockchain, several companies may process the same information in parallel and call each other's attention to key bits, thereby keeping themselves up to date on developing opportunities and warning each other of impending disasters. Other promises of blockchain – data richness, bandwidth, embedded computing – serve as complementary features to facilitate such real-time, distributed communication.

Timing, the second major benefit of virtual proximity, is critical for supply chain information. The captain of the *Titanic* knew his ship was headed into an iceberg; he just learned that information too late to adjust the big ship's course. Blockchain not only gets you information, it gets it to you quickly. It is one thing to learn that a supplier's plant is beyond capacity today. It is another to know that the plant will experience capacity problems tomorrow or next week. It's one thing to learn the names of two new suppliers that are working with one of your key partners. It is another to discover a short-term need for an additional supplier and that you should start talking to your key partner about possible candidates. Early warnings provide the opportunity to act on information yourself or to invest it back into the network. There are also benefits in the opposite flow. The network that filters information coming to you also directs, concentrates and legitimates information about you that's going to others.

> **Structural embeddedness** involves how relationships are configured or structured. This is the impersonal side of interactions.
>
> **Relational embeddedness** is the configuration of personal relationships developed through a history of interactions. It's the more personal element and involves the quality of the relationships rather than the structure.

The second important dimension common to all networks is relational embeddedness. Organizational theorists define relational embeddedness as the configuration of personal relationships developed through a history of interactions. It's the more personal element of embeddedness and involves the quality of the relationships rather than the structure. Relational embeddedness can involve several factors, including overlapping identities, solidarity or trust. According to Granovetter, the strength of the ties is based on a "combination of the amount of time, the emotional intensity, the intimacy (mutual confiding), and the reciprocity services which characterize the tie".

Scholars like to point out that structural embeddedness shapes the potential amount and range of resources to which someone in the firm has access. It is essential for identifying and understanding the patterns in the ways social capital is exchanged within networks and the channels used to transfer information. The stronger the structural embeddedness, the greater the available information about all the different parties within the network and the bigger the constraints on each party's behaviour.

Relational embeddedness, meanwhile, defines how much of this potential will be actualized. For instance, you and a competitor might have a common supplier and you both might have the same key contact within that organization. But let's say you grew up with that key contact, that she was maid of honour at your wedding, and that she is godmother to your children. Your relational embeddedness is most likely significantly stronger than your competition's.

Evolving dynamics

Structural and relational embeddedness are each different in different stages of a supply network's evolution. In general, supply networks evolve from fluid, dispersed constellations of companies, to more consolidated, rapidly expanding arrangements and then to shrinking, declining systems. At each stage, companies face different challenges and therefore blockchain will provide different benefits.

Fluid supply networks

Fluid supply networks, which are usually built by newly established, entrepreneurial firms, are characterized by scattered relationships with a very low rate of structural embeddedness. The new firm is engaged in exploration, which involves the development of new resources and new capabilities, trial and error, lack of well-defined industrial standards, and high technological uncertainty. In this stage, the production methods and systems are unsettled, the technological and the business concepts are emerging, and a common body of knowledge scarcely exists. The relationships are often random, the extent of relational embeddedness is minimal, and the number of structural holes is high. Demand also is embryonic and uncertain.

A fluid supply network, for example, could involve a startup that is forming partners to supply raw materials to make its product, as well as options for distributing the product with potential retailers.

In fluid networks, relationships are often weak and transient. They are arm's-length and often adversarial. Such transient relationships are mostly based on discrete transactions. Business deals are made through competitive bidding and aggressive price negotiations. The contacts are mostly short term, as in open commodity markets. With short-term gains as their primary focus, parties prefer to enforce and adhere to contractual terms. There is a high degree of ambiguity about the future of the relationship. There is also a high degree of supplier flexibility.

Say an entrepreneur wins a bid from a big retailer to supply a few thousands of garments. The entrepreneur may decide to buy textile from a European producer but have it dyed in Taiwan. He picks the

Figure 5.6 A fluid network over three quarters

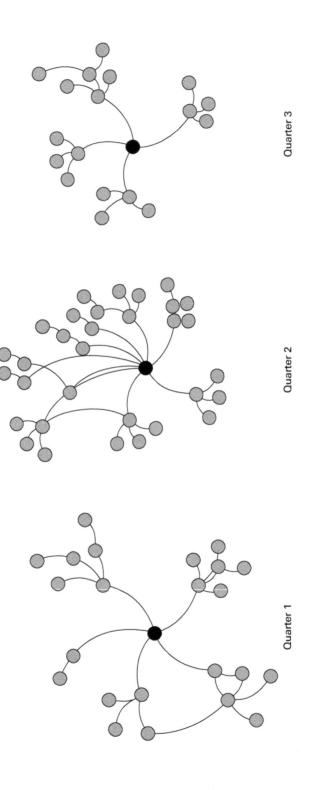

Quarter 1   Quarter 2   Quarter 3

textile and ships it to Taiwan. He knows that the best zippers and buttons come from Japanese manufacturers. He also knows that they manufacture them mostly in China. Then the entrepreneur has to determine the best place to make the garments, given quotas and labour conditions. Let's say it is Thailand. So, he has to reroute everything there. Because the retailer always needs quick delivery, the entrepreneur may divide the order across five factories in Thailand. The supply network is fluid because the entrepreneur is customizing everything to best meet the retailer's needs. Essentially, he dissects the manufacturing process into steps and looks for the best solution at each step.

In a typical fluid relationship, the buyer and supplier relate to each other based on their short-term preferences (for example, matching cost or delivery requirements). Because their interactions are mostly driven by short-term, discrete contracts, the partners would have only a casual understanding of each other's business strategies, needs, capabilities and operations. This fluid relationship can provide some advantages, particularly when it comes to sharing information. For instance, the supplier is likely to be exposed to many other partners and perspectives through its own network. The supplier will likely have other buyers and therefore be very adaptable in tackling different challenges. Through its relationship with such a supplier, the buyer can also have enhanced access to diverse perspectives.

If we take a snapshot of a fluid network from one quarter to the next, the pictures will be different (Figure 5.6). A fluid network may grow larger from one quarter to another and then become smaller as temporary suppliers leave.

Mature, rigid networks can have fluid, dynamic regions. For example, an established company may be exploring a new market or developing a new product or service. Kansas City Southern Railway, for instance, launched a blockchain pilot with a goal of improving the efficiency of a fluid relationship. In this case, they tested a blockchain to connect a shipper in Asia, a carrier (Maersk) and customs agents in Mexico and the United States. Kansas City Southern Railway works with the port operator and a local customs broker to help clear the freight, which involves approval through Mexico customs on the outbound and the US customs on the inbound. All these entities

Figure 5.7 Networks that grow from year to year

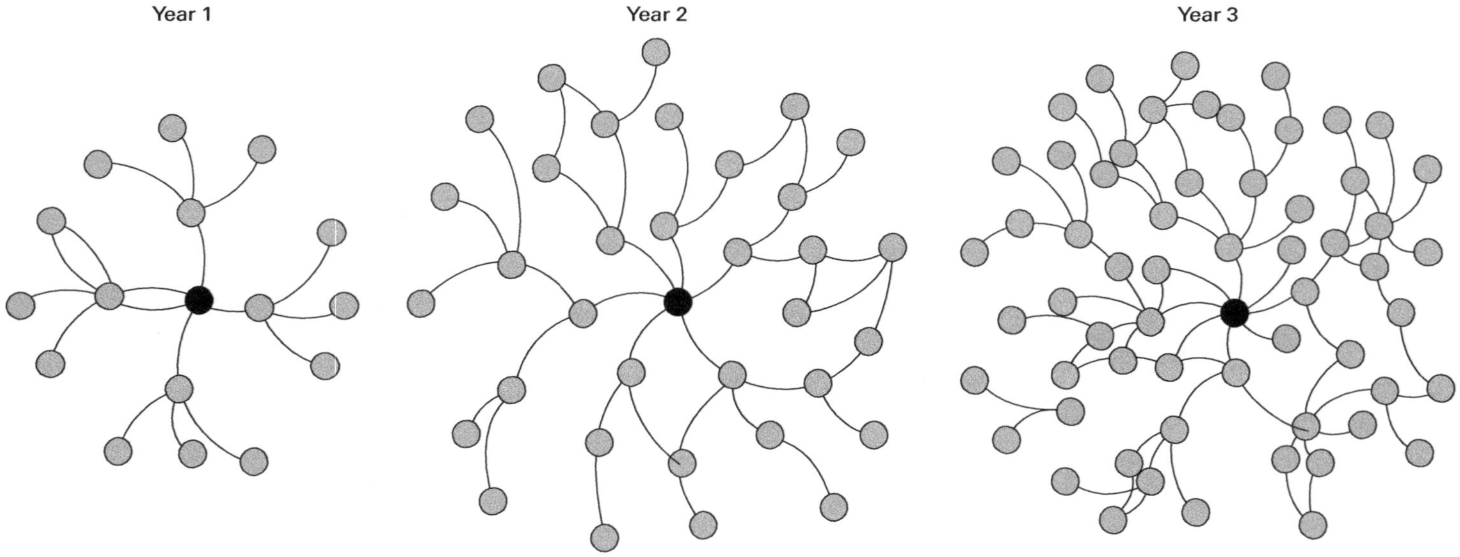

Year 1

Year 2

Year 3

are related to each other in a weak, transient way, meaning they don't depend on each other for survival. Efficiency in cost and lead times are important to Kansas City Southern Railway as it explores this new market.

Main goals in the fluid stage: Accumulation of a critical mass of assets, capabilities, and collaborations with firms within a network.

Challenges of the fluid stage: Extremely dispersed network structure. Structural holes. Mainly weak ties among disconnected firms. Production systems are unsettled and the business concepts are dispersed. Demand is uncertain.

Benefits of blockchain: Spanning structural holes. Effective connection with firms within a network. While it is very challenging to reach an agreement to establish blockchain-based data sharing with a transient partner, the benefits of such an arrangement can be huge.

Growing supply networks

The successful introduction of a new product or service to the market sets off the growth of the supply network. A firm establishes first-order relationships within its supply network, and structural embeddedness within the network increases. Companies begin to benefit from shared opportunities coupled with shared risks. This stage often comes with a critical mass of effective technological solutions and a high level of connectivity in the network, allowing complementing capabilities, knowledge and technology to benefit the network members. There is also the need for standardization as the firms strive to establish the common language and technical framework. The firms have common interests, which drives trustworthy collaborations and increases relational embeddedness. The winning solution becomes more about the higher systemic and collaborative efficiency than technological or innovative superiority.

Growing networks don't just grow the business of the companies involved, they grow in the number of companies involved. And as the number of links among the companies in the network grows, the networks become denser (Figure 5.7). Some supply networks grow rapidly, adding many new members each quarter. Often, however, this growth is more gradual and occurs over the course of years.

For example, many large retailers also have their own lines of products. Gone are the days when buyers just sat in their offices looking at samples; now they actively design and create products. The hard part is managing suppliers and the flow of parts and materials. This can be especially challenging with clothing, where demand is seasonal and things go out of style quickly. The easy approach is to place an order for finished goods and let the supplier worry about contracting for the raw materials. But if the supplier is too small to demand faster deliveries from its suppliers, the order may take months, not weeks. To shrink the delivery cycle, retailers now go upstream to organize production. The shorter production time gives the retailer extra time before committing to a fashion trend. For them, it is all about flexibility, response time, small production runs, small minimum-order quantities and the ability to shift directions with the trends.

Unlike fluid supply networks, growing supply networks are usually organized around a core of long-standing suppliers. Partners seek synchronization and the reduction of uncertainty. They want to develop common behavioural norms with their suppliers and a shared body of knowledge to achieve higher levels of process-based trust. Collaboration becomes longer and more frequent. The increasing relational embeddedness within the supply network leads to the need for shared vision, while also providing access to trustworthy information about the partners' quality and reliability. Moreover, previous collaborative experiences enhance the trust between the parties in their future interactions.

The firms now proceed from product innovation to process innovation in order to achieve economies of scale and scope. Groups of collaborating firms strive to increase sales.

The collaboration ties between firms have two major formats: sticky and gracious.

Sticky ties are close but adversarial. In a sticky relationship, the partners view each other as a necessary evil. The more powerful partner may change or modify the exchange to its own advantage. The weaker partner may often be forced into relation-specific investments and thus is put in a hostage position. The dominant party leans towards using adversarial tactics to seize a larger share of benefits at the cost of the weaker partner. At the same time, the weaker partner tries to "get even" via covert means and tactics.

Sticky relationships usually involve contractual disparities and unilateral demands. For example, the buyer can demand an aggressive cost reduction schedule. The increasing animosity is usually accompanied by a lack of shared information. This keeps the partners from building commitment and trust, regardless of how integrated they may be at the operational level. In some cases, buyers audit their suppliers to prevent them from earning extra profits. As one party gains at the expense of the other, this type of relationship lacks the synergy associated with mutual efforts to create surplus benefits and their fair distribution.

The sticky relationship does not always favour the more powerful party, because the weaker party can engage in covert retaliation. A supplier that has accumulated a good understanding of the buyer's operations and business needs, as well as the terms of their contract agreements, is well equipped to engage in covert opportunism with potentially substantive consequences. Such actions usually cannot be easily checked or monitored. For instance, the disadvantaged supplier may purposely withhold critical parts and key information or fail to follow through the quality procedures prescribed in the contract.

In contrast, gracious relationships are arm's-length but cooperative. The partners may not work together intensely but hold each other in high regard. They may engage in intermittent and short-term yet recurrent collaborations. Business deals might take place infrequently, but they occur in a spirit of friendship. The supplier in such a relationship is less reliant on the buyer and typically is resourceful and has diversified product offerings and a balanced customer base. Generally, both parties retain autonomy in their respective operations, while remaining positive towards each other.

Let's say a retailer is going to order several thousand garments, but has not decided on the style or the colours. In fashion, these decisions are made only five or six weeks before the retailer needs the order delivered. The gracious relationship would allow the retailer to reserve undyed fabric from the fabric supplier. The gracious retailer can also reserve capacity at the mills for the dyeing process on the understanding that they'll get the order. The retailer can say the same to the factories: "I don't know all the specs yet, but I have already organized the fabric and the dyeing, and the dyed fabric will be delivered to you on this date, and you'll have three weeks to produce the garments."

The supplier in these relationships may not do much work for the buyer overall, but it maintains an amicable disposition towards the buyer. While the buyer may see advantages in maintaining a tie with the resourceful supplier, it holds little leverage over the supplier, because the tie is weak. The supplier may have connections to various other companies, even to the buyer's rivals. Typically, the buyer would likely be in a holding pattern to see whether its link with this supplier will pay off in the future.

Interestingly, a supplier in such gracious relationships can be a great source of innovation for the buyer. Given the weak-tie relationship, the supplier has the potential to serve as a conduit for new ideas and market information. One of the true merits of gracious relationships is the high likelihood of introducing the buying firm to otherwise unconnected fields of businesses. That exposure to far-flung regions of the network or even totally different industries can potentially bring novel information or resources to the buyer.

Main goals in the growth stage: Acquisition of market share, definition of standards, norms, common practices and business concepts. Leveraging available network resources. Attainment of a strong position within the growing network. Achieving economies of scale and scope.

Challenges of the growth stage: Growing dependency on key suppliers. Structural holes.

Benefits of blockchain: Blockchain could reconfigure the supply network by connecting all the players through direct, virtual ties. This opens the door to economies of scale by enabling the firms to develop and promote shared interests and goals, shared behavioural standards, and even collectively watching out for those partners who choose to engage in opportunism.

Frank Yiannas points out, for instance, that blockchain could play a significant role in fighting fraud in the food industry. "Fraud in food is pretty big," he told us. "Right now, it's reported that there's more organic food being sold on the planet than is being produced. You've seen stories of fraud…. It's because there's not a lot of transparency in the food systems, so we're trying to solve for transparency issues that might deter fraud" (Yiannas, 2017).

One of Walmart's first pilots involved digitizing records in the pork supply chain in China. Information on the blockchain came from the farm, slaughter house, transportation trucks, Animal Product Quarantine Certificate Exchange, distribution centre, and store. By scanning the case labels, authorized workers could view purchase orders, shipping details, and even veterinary certificates – all documents that previously were handled with paper.

"If you start creating a more transparent, digitized supply chain using blockchain, you might uncover some things you didn't know that aren't good," Yiannas told us. "Some people will be afraid of getting into such systems because they're afraid of what they might uncover. But I think, on balance, knowing about them and being able to manage those risks is better than not knowing about them" (Yiannas, 2017).

Mature supply networks

The increasing relational embeddedness of the growth stage brings the supply network closer to the maturity stage, which is characterized by the focus on economies of scale and an efficient and low-cost collaborative environment. The beginning of the mature stage is marked by a shift from exploration and intense innovation to more exploitative activities that emphasize operational improvement. Operations are mostly stabilized and improvement becomes mostly incremental.

Because mature networks are often rigid, it becomes increasingly difficult for companies to adapt to changes in other industries or, most importantly, to shifts in consumer demand. Before cameras went digital and became part of smartphones, for example, Kodak was a household brand with an unparalleled dominance in its industry. At its height, Kodak controlled more than 80 per cent of the US photographic film market and about 50 per cent of the global market. For decades, Kodak operated a sizable worldwide system of manufacturing facilities and distribution networks. Through direct ownership or by keeping a major stake, the company controlled most parts of its supply chain, including raw materials such as chemicals. Now, after a collapse and a bankruptcy, Kodak is a shadow of what it used to be and it has sold off much of its former distribution network.

As consumers shift their preferences, a mature supply network always begins to disintegrate and decline, although maybe not at the speed of Kodak's demise. Sales volumes continuously decrease, and firms tend to maximize their exploitative efforts within the network while exploring alternative directions. In this phase, success depends on the ability to lead an efficient change in routines, to re-engineer processes and to alter the sources of competitive advantages. These objectives demand that all the partners look for new areas of activity and, therefore, new supply networks. This leads to an incremental decrease in the number of interactions within the network and a reduction in the frequency of ties among the collaborating members. As the number of members decreases, the structural embeddedness of the supply network typically decreases as well. The relational embeddedness, however, plays a more fundamental role as relationships become deep, stable and rigid.

Such relationships are usually closely coordinated and cooperative. They facilitate orderly, reliable flows of information and material, which can help parties align their relational goals and achieve operational objectives. Consequently, the buyer attains high consistency in product quality and lead time. In a deep buyer–supplier relationship, the two firms are closely synchronized in their operations through an extensive use of information technology. Typically, both parties dedicate a significant portion of their internal resources to the relationship, which allows efficient communications and coordinated production activities. They become highly dependent on each other, both operationally and strategically, and are less likely to engage in unilateral power plays and more likely to cooperate for mutual benefits. The cooperative behaviours lead to less conflict in communication and negotiations. By reducing relational uncertainty and boosting operational efficiency, the deep relationship provides stability to both parties.

Partners in a deep relationship, however, may experience diminishing returns. Their high sunk costs and vested interest in the relation can become so cohesive that they develop distorted perceptions of circumstances outside the relationship. This limits each partner's access to diverse perspectives. Both parties tend to cling to existing belief systems and replicate successful internal routines, even when the external business environment changes. Having invested in resources dedicated to the relationship, the supplier is particularly likely to resist change. Knowing it would be difficult for the buyer to find another supplier to make such investments, the supplier may even show complacency and begin to take the relationship for granted. Consequently, the supplier would likely become less enthusiastic about venturing out. From the buyer's perspective, the supplier would appear to be increasingly rigid and set in its ways.

Main goals in the mature stage: Maximizing the ability to exploit the current position. Exploring opportunities in other industries and markets.

Challenges of the mature stage: Dispersing and shrinking network with decreasing density. Shift in consumer preferences and decreasing demand.

Benefits of blockchain: Control over the existing supply ties and connecting with new networks to explore new opportunities. Ability to both increase the efficiency of existing processes through greatly improved visibility and experiment with new products or supply chain partners.

Table 5.1 Summary of goals, challenges and benefits in supply network stages

	Fluid	**Growing**	**Mature**
Goal	Critical mass of assets, capabilities, and collaborations	Market share, economies of scale and scope	Exploit existing and explore new opportunities
Challenges	Dispersed network, structural holes, and week ties	Dependency on key suppliers, structural holes	Dispersing/ shrinking network
Benefits of Blockchain	Span structural holes, gain advantages of data sharing with new transient partners	Reconfigure supply network	Governance of existing supply ties, explore new opportunities

Enabling versatile information flows

Everyone benefits when useful information flows efficiently between the different contacts in a network. Given the reality that supply chain networks are increasingly complex and dynamic, however, the challenge at any stage is to identify potential partners who can provide relevant information and to figure out the best way to access that information in a timely, trustworthy manner. Blockchain provides a potential solution because one of its unique benefits is its versatility in enabling and strengthening the flow of information across all types of network links. These links can range from open to closed and tightly controlled.

Some companies are very open and prefer to connect to partners who are open as well. For them, the supply network is an important source of knowledge and innovative ideas. These companies often benefit from the "information spillover" that happens when information is freely diffused. This is similar to an industry conference where an exchange of information among a few companies benefits all other network members who can connect and learn from what they hear.

Most connections in supply networks, however, are more restricted. They are usually governed by non-disclosure agreements or similar arrangements designed to ensure that only the specific parties benefit from information that is exchanged. Unlike the open connections, which are mostly weak ties, these connections involve stronger relationships and a tighter control over the exchanged information.

Blockchain can be easily configured to work for both types of connection. It can interconnect members in an open network and enable a higher rate of information diffusion, but it can also include coded access authorizations so that it works for partners who want more stringent controls and more secure, tighter communication policies.

Blockchain can curate the network itself by restricting access or curate the content that each member of the network can access. And it can work as well in a totally open network where everyone sees what everyone else has entered. Informational middlemen are in supply networks mostly because they provide a bridge that spans the informational structural holes. Blockchain can remove the middlemen and third parties from databases and data-sharing processes without compromising data robustness and integrity.

Finding structural holes

Most holes are pretty easy to find. Survey the landscape and look for places where the landscape is missing. When you see evidence of missing landscape, that's most likely a hole. Let's say, for instance, you've spent hours and hours working to develop a beautiful lawn for your family's home. You fertilized, watered, mowed, and attacked weeds with a vengeance that would make Genghis Khan proud. Then one day the gopher family moves in. They hunger for the grubs and earthworms beneath your grass, so they do what gophers do and tunnel their way towards brunch. Now your once manicured landscape is marked by a maze of missing landscape, otherwise known as holes.

Finding structural holes in your supply network isn't always so easy, because they are both structural and relational in nature. You might scan the landscape and see everything just as you think it should be, only to discover later that something key was missing – a gaping hole in a relationship or in the structure that was hidden beneath the surface or beyond your field of vision.

There are three common symptoms of a structural hole in your network. One, when you are aware that you don't know something valuable that may potentially affect your operations. Two, when you lack access to important information. For example, you know where your blind spot lies but you can't get through it. And three, when there's a relatively high cost to access the information. So, a structural hole usually means that information or data from the other end are valuable for you but accessing them is hard and/or costly.

McDonald's, for example, sources beef from several countries, including the United States, Australia, New Zealand and Canada. In the process of getting that beef from the farm to the burger you purchase, the meat goes through several intermediate distributors or carriers. The value of visibility and knowledge about the details of that journey – where it passed through and when – is high, especially if there is a problem with the beef. The faster and more precisely McDonald's can pinpoint the problem, the faster it can remove every lot that came from a problematic farm or that passed through an intermediary where it became contaminated.

This is a formidable task in the current supply chain network. During the 2013 horsemeat scandal in Europe, McDonald's addressed its customers' concerns by issuing a series of ads that clarified the provenance of its beef. It would have been much more effective if McDonald's could have said: "We know where each pound of our beef comes from. Our blockchain can show it in detail." They couldn't, because the structural holes in their supply network limited their ability to quickly access that information.

Kodak faces a similar challenge, because some of the chemicals used to produce film contain minerals that might originate in the conflict zones of the Democratic Republic of Congo (DRC) and adjoining countries. Kodak knows its products contain these minerals, but is often unable to determine their origins. This makes it hard to satisfy the Securities and Exchange Commission's disclosure rules for "conflict minerals" and customers who are concerned about this issue.

Like McDonald's, Kodak and many others, the problems you are trying to solve with a supplier may immediately cause you to start identifying who most likely knows something important or who has the critical data. But that person is typically a weak tie in your network. If it were a strong tie, you'd already have an established, continuous flow of information.

In Figure 5.8, for instance, Node A (black) represents you, while Node B (grey) represents your primary supplier, and the other nodes represent the various companies that supply your primary supplier. The only way for you to know what is going on among the supplier nodes is to rely on Node B's information. Node B is most likely your strong tie, and there is already a continuous data flow between you. Your knowledge about the other supplier nodes, however, is only as good as Node B decides it to be. And for many companies, as would be the case for McDonald's and Kodak, the cluster of suppliers and their sub-suppliers is far more numerous, complex and dynamic than in this simplified example.

Figure 5.8 A simple network connection

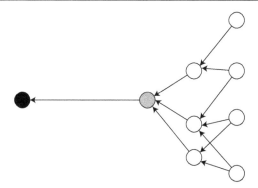

The other suppliers may possess valuable knowledge, but there is no point in establishing an expensive EDI connection with any of them, because you don't know how long they will be there. Knowing that someone else has valuable expertise is important, but their knowledge is really helpful only if they are accessible. If you've identified missing information as valuable and you know you lack access to it, then you still need to consider the cost of bridging the structural hole.

This cost is related to the difficulty of access, but there are other factors. If there is no information technology link between Node A and any of the other suppliers beyond Node B, for instance, the cost of obtaining information from them is higher in terms of money, time or effort. Obligations that result from an exchange of information also can be a cost. Asking someone on the other side of a structural hole for significant information, in other words, can result in obligations that come with the norms of reciprocity.

It's within the context of structural holes that blockchain truly shines. Most companies only seek and rely on accessible information, but blockchain expands the list of what can be easily accessible by eliminating the structural holes.

You can span the structural hole by establishing a blockchain-based information link with a supplier of your supplier. Ideally, it should be densely connected with other companies in its cluster. By establishing a blockchain-based connection with the right supplier of Node B (the dotted arrow in Figure 5.9 from Nodes C to A), for instance, you increase your access to important information beyond what you were getting from your direct supplier (Node B). Now, you also have access to key information from your supplier's supplier, but also from that supplier's suppliers – the three nodes located on the "other side" that are linked to Node C. Thus, you increase your knowledge about information that previously was only available indirectly. The ability of blockchain to establish a cheap, secure and effective data channel between you and another company is at the core of this advantage.

Figure 5.9   Spanning a structural hole

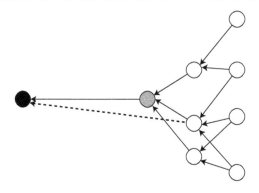

We mentioned earlier that blockchain is more of a foundational technology than a disruptive technology, and most of the disruption it's causing is emerging from the associated hype. But its ability to span structural holes in a cost-effective way gives it disruptive potential.

In *The Innovator's Dilemma*, Harvard Professor Clayton Christensen distinguishes between disruptive innovations and sustaining innovations. A sustaining innovation brings an incremental, steady improvement. Most of the current debate about blockchain revolves around whether it is better than the existing technology or databases that can serve the same purposes. As we've already pointed out, it's indeed hard to find significant ways in which blockchain is better than the existing solutions. Therefore, it is hard to see its potential as a sustaining innovation.

According to Christensen, a disruptive technology often starts out as inferior in some attributes that are valued by major, mainstream partners such as Node B in our example. Such partners probably see blockchain as unattractive, even undesirable, since they stand to lose some control over the information you get about things happening "on the other side". When you are focused on Node B, you may overlook the possibility and value of establishing links with other, indirect suppliers.

Blockchain, in fact, offers a package of attributes that work quite well with indirect partners. For example, a blockchain-based connection can be quickly and relatively cheaply established between any two companies. Without the need to install and configure a more expensive and less flexible solution like an EDI, blockchain can connect indirect partners about whom you have relatively no knowledge. This can open up entirely new possibilities of broader visibility, deeper learning and better situation awareness. Other companies may step in and start developing and exploring the value of links with indirect suppliers. Such links are rare because they are costly and largely don't bring much benefit. With blockchain, however, more and more companies will be building such links. In this way, blockchain may become an established technology making a weak tie stronger or an indirect tie direct. Blockchain may then invade the territory occupied by traditional technologies used between direct, major partners.

As you can see, network theory provides a great deal of insight into how blockchain can be used in increasingly complex, increasingly dynamic supply chain ecosystems. But how will those factors impact specific areas of supply chain management within those ecosystems? The remaining chapters in this section will answer that question by looking more deeply into blockchain's potential effect on five interconnected components of supply chain management: sustainable supply chain management, inventory management, demand management, supply management and transportation management.

Chain links: Key points from this chapter

- Two seismic transformations are sweeping through global supply chains. First, supply chains are becoming increasingly complex. Second, supply chains and operations are getting increasingly dynamic.

- The shifts from simple supply chains to supply networks within complex and dynamic ecosystems will make network theory an increasingly important component in supply chain management. So, network theory plays a key role in understanding and implementing blockchain solutions.

- Structural embeddedness involves how relationships are configured or structured. This is the impersonal side of the interactions.

- Relational embeddedness is the configuration of personal relationships developed through a history of interactions. It's the more personal element of embeddedness and involves the quality of the relationships rather than the structure.

- The more you can close the gap in the structure that connects your two networks – in other words, create better access to other members in the other network – the better your information and resources and the greater likelihood that you can use your network connection as a competitive advantage.

- The virtual proximity allowed by blockchain provides major benefits for access and timing of information sharing.

- Supply networks typically evolve from fluid, dispersed constellations of companies to more consolidated, rapidly expanding arrangements and then to shrinking, declining systems. At each stage, companies face different challenges, blockchain will provide different benefits.

- There are three common symptoms of a structural hole in your network. One, when you are aware that you don't know something valuable that may potentially affect your operations. Two, when you lack the access to important information. And three, when there's a relatively high cost to access the information.

- Blockchain can connect indirect partners about whom you have relatively no knowledge. This can open up entirely new possibilities of broader visibility, deeper learning and better situation awareness.

Reference

Yiannas, F (2017) Interview with the authors for this book, 22 December

Sustainable supply chain management

06

Two transportation moguls from competing companies shook hands in 1989 while riding in a passenger car attached to a freight train as it rolled across middle America. The agreement they struck that afternoon – laughed at by some and dismissed as insignificant by others – ended up reshaping the freight transportation industry.

The "strategic alliance" between J B Hunt, founder of J B Hunt Transport, and Mike Haverty, then the president of the Santa Fe Railway Company, produced a first-of-its-kind intermodal transportation venture, and it changed the trajectory of both companies by putting them on the leading edge of a billion-dollar strategy.

It was one of those ideas that seems obvious in hindsight – use the fleet of a major trucking company to move containers from a shipper to the railroad yard, load the containers onto a train for a cross-country run, then use the trucking company's fleet again on the other end for final-mile delivery. No one had tried it before, mainly because no one thought players from the highly competitive and often adversarial railroad and trucking industries could work together without, well, trying to run over each other along the way. The alliance, however, proved hugely successful. It brought reliable service to the railroad company, while reducing its reliance on brokers. It reduced the trucking company's need for long-haul drivers, who were (and still are) in short supply. And it opened the doors to new business and growth for both companies.

It also would have scored the companies points on their corporate sustainability reports – although such a thing was largely unheard of at the time. The side benefit that Hunt and Haverty might not have immediately considered when they originally agreed to their deal was the increase in intermodal reduced congestion on the United States' crowded highways. Lowering J B Hunt's greenhouse gas emissions and its carbon footprint made the arrangement considerably friendlier to the environment.

Over the past 30 years, a company's environmental impact – and its overall approach to sustainability – has become increasingly important to everyone connected to supply chain management. Sustainability today, in fact, is mostly seen as a supply chain management responsibility. A sustainable firm is not possible unless the supply chain is sustainable. So, any technology that promises to improve sustainability throughout the supply chain is a technology that should interest supply chain managers.

We recognize, of course, that *sustainability* is one of those trendy terms that means something different to just about everyone who uses it, so let's align on a common definition as it applies to supply chain management. Craig Carter and Dale Rogers, in a seminal 2008 article in the *International Journal of Physical Distribution & Logistics Management*, defined sustainable supply chain management (SSCM) as "the strategic, transparent integration and achievement of an organization's social, environmental, and economic goals in the systemic coordination of key interorganizational business processes for improving long-term economic performance" (Carter and Rogers, 2008).

That's more than an academic mouthful, but it's darn accurate. The big idea is the integration of "social, environmental, and economic" responsibilities, with the underlying assertion that SSCM actually creates value for the various organizations involved. And, indeed, empirical findings indicate that balancing environmental, social and economic performance leads to improved operational efficiency and cost reductions, quality, compliance, risk mitigation, supply chain security, company image, health and safety standards for workers, market growth and revenue generation. (See Golicic and Smith, 2013; Hollos, Blome and Foerstl, 2012; Pagell and Wu, 2009; Pagell, Wu and Wasserman, 2010; Reuter *et al*, 2010; and Zhu, Sarkis and Lai, 2013.)

Many companies have rushed to adopt this broader view of sustainability like it was an adorable puppy. Consider that the primary emphasis of sustainability reports in 1999 was on environmental issues. By 2004, about 68 per cent of the Global 250 firms generated a separate annual sustainability report that considered environmental, social and economic issues. Additionally, 80 per cent of these reports discussed supply-chain-related issues.

Environmental and social impacts occur across the supply chain, and, in general, the biggest impacts are on raw materials – farms, mines and other suppliers where we have the least amount of visibility – and in areas related to transportation. More than 20 per cent of global greenhouse gas emissions are made by about 2,500 of the largest global companies, according to the 2011 Carbon Disclosure Project, and their supply chains are responsible for a major proportion of emissions resulting from corporate operations.

The challenge, as we illustrated previously, is that today's supply chains are complex and dynamic ecosystems. Purchasing firms lack visibility into all the different layers of their supply chain, thus they lack information, which means they can't do accurate, complete analysis. Furthermore, they lack control over the sustainability practices of their suppliers, but, in many cases, they shoulder the blame for any sustainability-related problems that arise from those suppliers. In this regard, SSCM is not just about operational efficiencies – it's also about marketing and public relations.

Some companies, of course, eagerly brand themselves as eco-friendly and sustainable. Patagonia, for instance, mails its outdoor clothing and gear in recyclable bags rather than bulky boxes and regularly reviews its supply chain to identify and cut financial and environmental waste. It's also among more than 2,600 companies in 60-plus countries that are certified "B Corps" and, therefore, are "legally required to consider the impact of their decisions on their workers, customers, suppliers, community, and the environment" (Bcorporations.net, 2018).

Other companies are doing some amazing things in sustainability (based on our research and interacting with them), but are unwilling to let the public know about it, yet. They are hesitant to put themselves out there because that type of branding often makes them an easy target if and when something goes wrong, even if that "something" is outside of their control. The negative backlash is much greater relative to competitors who don't brand themselves as sustainable, and companies with big, thick reports on all the ways they "do good" aren't immune to criticism when their suppliers go off the sustainability rails.

When troublesome working conditions were exposed at the Foxxcon factories in Japan that assemble smartphones and tablets, companies like Apple took the heat. When Indonesian-based palm oil producer Sawit Sumbermas Sarana was accused of deforestation practices, companies like Unilever were expected to hold them accountable. Go to Nestlé's website and you can find a 113-page report on how the company is creating shared value, enhancing quality of life, and contributing to a healthier future. But go to listverse. com and you can read about "10 Outrageous Nestlé Scandals".

The main issue with all this is that no company of any significant size can know *everything* that is going on in the supply chain, and this is where blockchain can help the most. Blockchain promises to hold employees and, ultimately, businesses and their supply chains accountable by providing visibility into a tamper-resistant ledger.

Sustainability, of course, is an issue for all areas of supply chain management, so the potential of blockchain on SSCM is something we will discuss in some specific ways throughout the next few chapters. But it's worth noting that the World Economic Forum published a report in September 2018 that outlined 65 ways it claimed blockchain, if used responsibly, could "fix global environmental challenges". In releasing their report, the WEF's Sheila Warren pointed out that blockchain is "still a nascent technology", but said, "Now is the right time for stakeholders to work together to ensure the development of responsible blockchain solutions that are good for people and the planet" (World Economic Forum, 2018).

The report goes on to suggest that blockchain can be used to have a positive effect on climate change, biodiversity and conservation, healthy oceans, water security, clean air, and weather and disaster resilience. How so? Well, the report provides a laundry list of ideas and use cases that are being tested – from peer-to-peer renewable energy-trading systems to digital data platforms to tracking invasive species for disease control to decentralized disaster insurance platforms. Many of the ideas are clearly achievable using methods that don't involve blockchain. But in many cases, blockchain provides either the means to kick-start a positive initiative or, in some cases, a potential solution that wasn't there before.

In general, the solutions align with all the reasons we are sharing throughout this book. WEF categorizes them in five themes (Herweijer *et al*, 2018):

- enabling decentralized systems;
- peer-to-peer trading of natural resources or permits;
- supply chain monitoring and origin tracking;
- new financing models, including democratizing investment;
- realization of non-financial value, including natural capital.

For supply chain managers, these potential solutions to sustainability issues will play out across the many other aspects of planning and executing supply chain strategies in inventory management, demand management, supply management and transportation management. So, that's where we'll turn our attention next.

Chain links: Key points from this chapter

- Sustainability is mostly seen as a supply chain management responsibility.

- In supply chain management, sustainability centres around creating value by achieving social, environmental and economic goals.

- Environmental and social impacts occur across the supply chain; in general, the biggest impacts are on raw materials and in areas related to transportation.

- Sustainable supply chain management is not just about operational efficiencies; it's also about marketing and public relations.

- Blockchain promises to hold employees and, ultimately, businesses and their supply chains accountable by providing visibility into its tamper-resistant ledger.

- A World Economic Forum report suggests that blockchain can be used to have a positive effect on climate change, biodiversity and conservation, healthy oceans, water security, clean air, and weather and disaster resilience.

References

Bcorporations.net (2018) A Global Community of Leaders. bcorporation.net

Carter, C and Rogers, D (2008) A framework of sustainable supply chain management: moving toward new theory, *International Journal of Physical Distribution & Logistics Management*, **38**, pp 360–87, 10.1108/09600030810882816

Herweijer, C *et al* (2018) Building Block(chain)s for a Better Planet, *World Economic Forum*, 14 September. www.weforum.org/reports/building-block-chain-for-a-better-planet (archived at perma.cc/4A7T-23NV)

World Economic Forum (2018) Report: More than 65 Ways Blockchain Technology Can Fix Global Environmental Challenges, *World Economic Forum*, 14 September. www.weforum.org/press/2018/09/report-more-than-65-ways-blockchain-technology-can-fix-global-environmental-challenges/ (archived at perma.cc/A27S-PF5Y)

Inventory management 07

If you've worked in supply chain management for very long, then you are no doubt familiar with the bullwhip effect. You not only know what it is, but you've experienced it. Business students learn about this concept early in their academic journey, and practitioners deal with it almost daily. And while the bullwhip effect causes problems in just about every sector of supply chain management, the most direct correlations occur around the management of inventory. These challenges are accentuated by the advent of more complicated and dynamic networks. Because of this, blockchain's potential for reducing the bullwhip effect becomes an intriguing possibility for anyone managing inventories.

Because we work daily with college students, we find that an easy way to illustrate the bullwhip effect is with what we call the "beer game". Now, there's no actual beer involved in the beer game. That's a disappointment to some and a relief to others. The beer game is a classic management exercise that illustrates one of the most challenging realities of supply chain networks. If you want to toast a pint along the way, well, that's up to you. But we use poker chips in this game to represent cases of beer. It's less expensive and doesn't require taxis or designated drivers to get people home when the game is over.

There are five players in this simulation, each representing a different link in the supply chain – a retailer, a distributor, a wholesaler, a brewery (or factory) and a raw materials provider (Figure 7.1). Each participant places orders from the player directly downstream in the supply chain, but the order slip is their only form of communication. So, the retailer fills out a slip and passes it to the distributor who then fills out a slip and passes it to the wholesaler and so on. The orders then are filled using the poker chips – an order of four cases of beer, for example, would be filled with four poker chips.

Figure 7.1   Beer game

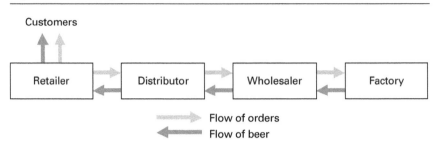

Customers

Retailer   Distributor   Wholesaler   Factory

Flow of orders
Flow of beer

Just like with any business, the players want to minimize costs and maximize customer service. Thus, the objective is to minimize the amount of pseudo beer any player is holding at one time so that the beer remains fresh – because who likes stale beer, right? And as in real life, each link in the chain must wait for orders to be filled and each link eventually experiences inventory build-ups or shortages.

It sounds easy enough, and it always starts off with very few problems. The simulation begins with the retailer ordering four cases. More often than not, each link in the chain adds a little to the order to provide some cushion. So, the distributor might order five cases from the wholesaler, who might order six from the brewery, who might order enough raw materials for seven cases.

The big shift, however, comes a few weeks (rounds) into the game when we have the retailer increase her order to eight cases. Each player responds by increasing their orders, again adding a small cushion. It only takes a few weeks for each player to run out of inventory because of delays in the fulfilment process. The players inevitably grow frustrated with each other and their natural reaction is to order even more. Around Week 20, however, the supply begins to catch up with the orders and cases of beer start pouring in to each player in the chain. Inventory builds as back-orders are filled. Every player in the game stops placing orders, which creates new frustrations throughout the supply network.

Here's the reality the players discover: little ripples create big ripples. In other words, small changes in demand (little ripples) create chaos (big ripples) throughout a supply chain.

Jay Wright Forrester, a pioneer of systems dynamics at the Massachusetts Institute of Technology, first described this as the

Figure 7.2 Beer game 2

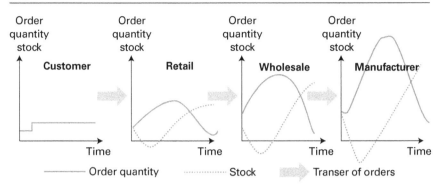

bullwhip effect back in the early 1960s. Forrester developed this model after conversations with General Electric managers about the fluctuations they were experiencing in areas like production, inventories, staffing and profit.

David Lane and John Sterman, who featured Forrester in a chapter of the book, *Profiles in Operations Research*, said Forrester noticed that the GE managers responded in a "locally rational fashion to the incentives and information they faced," but that the resulting policies, "sensible and rational from the perspective of the managers at each decision point, led to substantial amplification of perturbations in orders, and instability for the system as a whole" (Lane and Sterman, 2011).

Perhaps the most well-known example of the bullwhip effect involves nappies. Several years ago, Procter & Gamble noticed sales of its Pampers branded baby's nappies were fluctuating far more than they could attribute to any changes in birth rates. These fluctuations were causing problems as the little wiggles created bigger wiggles throughout the supply chain.

The cause? It began when Walmart ran a special on the nappies, creating an artificial demand. Everyone throughout the supply chain responded by increasing their orders. But parents stocked up on the discounted nappies, and the demand dipped accordingly. This created a glut of inventory. Suppliers overcorrected and, as demand began to pick back up, the shelves were soon empty. Parents then turned to other brands to cover their babies' bottoms. When the companies investigated the fluctuations, they realized they were experiencing the bullwhip effect. One of the reasons Walmart shifted to its "everyday low prices" model, in fact, was to prevent those types of fluctuations.

Price discounts are just one contributor to the bullwhip effect. Another is known as "demand signal processing", which involves rational ordering decisions by buyers who over-respond to fluctuations in downstream demand. They see any fluctuation as part of a long-term trend in demand, which can cause them to include safety stock that then contributes to the distortion of the demand signal. Buyers are also prone to over-order in anticipation of shortages.

Regardless, the bullwhip effect results in increased inventory carrying costs, higher prices for customers, lower margins for suppliers and increased uncertainty about true demand patterns.

Even though managers and academics have been aware of the bullwhip effect for decades, it remains one of the biggest challenges in operational efficiencies for supply chain practitioners, especially as supply chains grow more complex ecosystems with more and more factors that can trigger bullwhip reactions in all sorts of directions. So, it's worth repeating: the idea that blockchain technology might solve or significantly reduce its impacts is reason to celebrate.

The way to minimize the little ripples/big ripples of the bullwhip effect is by creating trusted synchronization. When you boil it down, the bullwhip effect occurs because the participants throughout the supply chain lack real-time information they can trust about the demands for the products they are buying and selling. Most companies use existing technologies such as EDI to track information about products as they move through supply chains. Despite huge investments in enterprise supply chain software, however, they still have limited visibility into where products are at any given moment.

Point-to-point messaging systems often are out of sync and only move data from one point in the supply chain to another. That worked OK for large, vertically integrated companies, but, again, today's supply chains aren't so static. Modern supply networks consist of hundreds of firms from different industries. As a result, supply chain leaders have to make decisions based on a large number of factors from multiple dimensions and perspectives. Complex interconnections between multiple suppliers, manufacturers, assemblers, distributors and retailers have become the new normal in modern supply networks. Decisions, however, are often still based on linear buyer–supplier connections and non-complex assumptions such as static environments and fixed behaviours. But webs of supply networks with multiple players in the ecosystems now demand flexibility, versatility and nimbleness to respond to ever-changing demands and product life cycles.

Melanie Nuce, a senior vice president of corporate development for GS1 US, is among those who can see how blockchain offers the possibility of real-time, accurate insight into information about products as they move throughout the ecosystems of modern supply networks:

> EDI was really peer-to-peer. I would send a manufacturer a purchase order, and they would send me a ship notice. But then the carrier would separately send me a shipment status notification that the manufacturer rarely saw, and the freight invoice would only go between the two parties. But (with blockchain) you're getting everyone involved in this conversation at the same time without having to build additional connectivity over and over again. You're getting much more discreet, physical event tracking that ties more closely to the products than these very disparate physical and information supply chains we've seen in the past. (Nuce, 2017)

This not only figures to reduce the negative results of the bullwhip effect, but leaders such as Frank Yiannas see potential in blockchain to create sort of a reverse bullwhip effect. Before leaving Walmart for a deputy commissioner position with the FDA, he told us:

> We have a pretty big supply chain and Walmart's known for being pretty good at this. But little tweaks and improvements in the supply chain or flow result in big benefits for businesses and the consumer. Just removing a couple of hours here and there in the way a strawberry moves from farm to table, that's a day or two of shelf life you give back to the consumer. That's a reduction in food waste, better quality of products... So, we shouldn't think we have the most efficient supply chain. There's still plenty to optimize about the way food flows from farm to table. (Yiannas, 2017)

Blockchain has the potential to improve several other aspects of inventory management. For instance, using blockchain to reduce inventories would provide a significant benefit by improving a company's return on assets.

The technology can also have a positive impact on the planning, forecasting, budgeting and staffing required to manage costs and services associated with inventory. For example, consider blockchain's effect on cycle stock – the expected amount of inventory used between replenishments. The more frequent the replenishments, the lower the amount of cycle stock. One of the expenses associated with replenishments is "invoice match failures". But blockchain can help reduce or eliminate those failures.

Invoice match failures occur because companies must make sure that invoices match the original order and the receiving document. When they don't match, the accounts payable department investigates to reconcile the differences, and those reconciliations can take lots of time. These failures don't occur with every order, of course, but there is a certain probability of them occurring with every order. Thus, the expected cost of an invoice match failure per order is a fixed cost. The higher this fixed cost, the fewer orders you want to place in a given year. That means the optimal amount of inventory that you order each time increases, which increases your average annual cycle stock.

A blockchain would make the reconciliations relatively quick and easy. In fact, incorporating a smart contract within the blockchain could eliminate the need to do a reconciliation. Smart contracts are programming embedded in a blockchain database that automatically trigger specified actions based on the transactions that take place. They are an "if/then" algorithm that the blockchain can execute without the need for human intervention. Using blockchain technology to quickly and accurately reconcile inventory orders can reduce cycle stock by lowering the costs associated with invoice match failures and thereby lowering overall ordering costs. Since blockchain technology, including smart contracts, can reduce or eliminate the expected cost of an invoice match failure, a company can place more frequent orders, thus reducing the annual cycle stock holding cost and quantity. Furthermore, reducing or eliminating invoice match failures could allow organizations to reduce the size of their accounts payable departments.

Smaller optimal order quantities also have additional implications for other aspects of logistics: a smaller quantity of units might be shipped per shipment 1) requiring a larger variety of assortment to be shipped in order to maintain full truckloads; 2) if truckload is not the mode used, then the demand for modes optimal for smaller shipments will grow and small-parcel shipments should grow (they have already been growing due to e-commerce); 3) pallet configuration may need to accommodate a wider variety of assortment per pallet; and 4) packaging may need to change because the optimal number of units per case may decrease.

Who would think that a reduction in or the elimination of invoice match failures could have such economy-wide effects? And we're only discussing the impact on one of the ordering costs, so just think of the overall effect of blockchain and smart contracts as we tackle each of the costs associated with orders. Also, as the example illustrates, the implications of blockchain and smart contracts can be subtle and nuanced; consequently, it is very easy to underestimate the magnitude and breadth of the impact of such changes.

Safety stock is another type of inventory that will likely see an impact from blockchain technology. Safety stock is extra inventory that is held to deal with uncertainty, primarily demand uncertainty and lead time uncertainty. If demand is highly uncertain or isn't visible, then more safety stock is needed to ensure a company doesn't run out of inventory. Walmart's provision of point of sale (POS) data is one way the retailer provides demand visibility to suppliers, thus reducing the suppliers' needs for safety stock. That visibility also allows for better planning of transportation and warehouse labour, thus reducing many other costs as well.

Blockchain technology could be used to further reduce demand uncertainty. Imagine a blockchain where every block recording a transaction showed the current number of units sold at every point in the supply network, along with forecasts based on a variety of forecasting models and a selection of the best forecasts based on AI. So, the block could include information such as: 1) 24 units sold yesterday; 2) 13 units sold so far today; 3) average units sold per day over the past week is 19; 4) forecasting model X predicts 21 units will be sold today; 5) forecasting model Y predicts that 17 units will be sold today …; n) forecasting model n predicts that 18 units will be sold today; and $n+1$) the AI-based forecast selection is 20 units. These blocks could be permissioned to all those in the blockchain who could improve planning based on the information.

It might seem that all you need is the AI-based forecast selection, but, unfortunately, that is not the case. Humans still need to be involved because we have not perfected the methods of selecting the "best" forecast. If that ever happens, we can completely take the human element out of forecasting, but we are not even close to that solution. Nevertheless, what we're suggesting here will still reduce safety stock in the supply chain even if it doesn't reduce labour very extensively. In addition, and possibly more importantly, it has great potential for reducing the number of out-of-stocks in the supply chain for the same reasons it reduces the need for safety stock.

Not only does safety stock guard against demand uncertainty, but it also guards against lead time uncertainty. If demand is completely certain but lead time – the time between when you place an order and when you receive the inventory and make it available for sale – is uncertain, then you need safety stock to reduce the frequency of out-of-stock occurrences. For example, suppose you always sell exactly five units of a particular item every day, you place an order from the supplier for five more units at the end of the day and receive them the next morning just before you open. In this case, demand and lead time are both certain and known and there is no need for safety stock. Now suppose that periodically the inventory is not received in the morning, but rather it arrives the following morning. In this case, you might want to keep more than five units on hand for the instances when this longer lead time occurs. This is a simple example, but it helps illustrate why lead time uncertainty is just as big of a problem as demand uncertainty and why they both drive the need for safety stock.

So, not only does blockchain have the potential to reduce demand uncertainty, but it can also reduce lead time uncertainty. Going back to the example where each block contained sales and forecasting information, those blocks could also include lead time information:

1) the time the order was received at a location in the supply chain, 2) the time between when the order was shipped from the upstream location to the current location, 3) the average time between locations, 4) the variance in time between locations, 5) the time between the origin location and the current location, and so on. Again, every permissioned entity in the supply chain could have visibility and thus reduce the lead time uncertainty and the need for safety stock.

Chain links: Key points from this chapter

- The bullwhip effects results in increased inventory carrying costs, higher prices for customers, lower margins for suppliers and increased uncertainty about true demand patterns. The idea that blockchain technology might solve or significantly reduce its impacts is reason to celebrate.

- Blockchain offers the possibility of real-time, accurate insight into information about products as they move through the ecosystems of modern supply networks. This not only figures to reduce the negative results of the bullwhip effect, but potentially creates a sort of reverse bullwhip effect.

- Using blockchain to reduce inventories would provide a significant benefit by improving a company's return on assets. The technology also can have a positive impact on the planning, forecasting, budgeting and staffing required to manage costs and services associated with inventory.

References

Lane, D and Sterman, J (2011) *Profiles in Operations Research*, written, compiled and edited by Arjang A Assad and Saul I Gass, Springer, New York

Nuce, M (2017) Interview with the authors for this book, 1 August

Yiannas, F (2017) Interview with the authors for this book, 22 December

Demand management

08

A woman we know flipped through the pages of a department store's advertising circular not long ago, and her eyes lit up when she came across a pair of red shoes. These weren't just any pair of red shoes. They were *the* red shoes. She had been looking for this style in this colour for more than a year. Not only had she now found them, but they were on sale!

She went to the department store that very afternoon, purse and debit card in hand. She found a reasonably close parking spot and nearly floated her way into the store and down its freshly waxed floors towards the shoe department. Hundreds of pairs of shoes in dozens of styles greeted her there, and on any other day she might have browsed through them in search of a bargain. Today, however, she was on a mission for the red shoes of her dreams. There was only one problem: the store didn't have the shoes. Not in red. Not in any colour.

Academics like to debate what is or isn't demand management, but this consumer could not have cared less about the supply chain management labels that might have been at play. All she cared about was that she had wasted a trip across town and was going home without her new red shoes. The department store, meanwhile, lost out on a sale and created a bad consumer experience that very well could have been shared across her social media platforms.

The purpose of this chapter isn't to argue about the definition of demand management. We recognize that the various parts of supply chain management are interconnected and can be sliced and diced in many different ways depending on who is wielding the knife. But in our view, everything about the shoe story connects to demand management.

The shoes might have been out of stock because of poor sales forecasting, which is the heart of all supply chain issues and most certainly the heart of managing demand. If the forecast was accurate, the planning based on that forecast might have been messed up, perhaps because of breaks in their sales and operations planning (S&OP) processes. Or perhaps they simply didn't execute to the plan. Regardless, it's all part of demand management. It's a classic example of demand side not coordinating with supply side. Marketing goes out and promotes, but it didn't ensure that the supply could be made available.

So, the question is this: if blockchain had been used by the retailer and its partners for the purpose of better demand management, could that consumer have got her shoes (or perhaps never have got the misleading circular)? Probably so, because blockchain figures to provide positive solutions across the board for demand management.

Demand management, in simple terms, is the creation of a coordinated flow of demand across the supply chain and its markets. It includes the traditional marketing activities, but it attempts to coordinate flow of demand across the supply chain (demand planning) by starting with a deep understanding of the consumer demand and aligning the planning and replenishment processes to actual consumption and consumer demand (S&OP). It provides incentives for supply chain members to participate in the demand planning processes, and it all starts with sales forecasting management. Blockchain provides the opportunity to significantly advance the impact of each of these areas in demand management.

Collaborative planning

Historically, as the bullwhip effect reveals, errors in sales forecasting regarding demand – and thus orders and inventory – are amplified at each upstream tier in the supply chain when disconnected supply chain members are operating independently.

This can be massive. For example, consider an overly simplified supply chain where the end-user demand is 10,000 units (Mentzer and Moon, 2004). The retailer, being excellent at forecasting sales, predicts the end-user demand to be 10,000 units. But because they do not know demand with certainty, they add 10 per cent for safety stock (based on historical experiences of fluctuating demand and not wanting to be left out of stock). The retailer then places an order for 11,000 units (the forecasted 10,000, plus 1,000 safety stock). The wholesaler independently forecasts and thus assumes consumer demand must be 11,000 units instead of 10,000 units. They also add 10 per cent for safety stock, and therefore place an order for 12,100 units (the forecasted 11,000 units plus 1,100 safety stock) from the manufacturer. This same pattern continues to the manufacturer, who places an order for 13,310 units to its Tier 1 supplier, which in turn places an order from its supplier for 14,640 units. Each member in this simplified supply chain really only needs 10,000 units plus 1,000 units of safety stock. But because they are not communicating effectively, the total error is 110.5 per cent, or the corresponding unnecessary safety stock of 7,050 units.

This example represents the traditional approach to demand management, where the marketing functions in companies are tasked with creating demand (promotional programmes, campaigns and price discounts) for various products, but little is shared with other companies in the supply chain. As we can see, this creates colossal challenges in planning and executing across the supply chain.

As we noted in the chapter on inventory management, one of the ways retailers can mitigate the bullwhip effect in the above example is by using point of sale (POS) data to provide visibility of sales across the supply chain. But this approach is still limited. For instance, suppose POS updates occur at the end of each day (not too uncommon in best-in-class companies). The following day, the transactions and inventory positions are analysed to create new purchase orders. On the third day, the supplier analyses the purchase order, aligns with available supply, and then signals a ship date. In the case where the supplier has available supply, it ships to the distribution centre on Day 4.

Even though it assumes a lot (like strong analyses on each of those days and available supplies), this is impressive compared to the historical supply chain demand planning and execution. But now imagine this process on blockchain, which can enable the real-time transfer of this sales information instead of waiting for daily refresh of POS sales. In one day (or less), the transaction and inventory position data that are available on the block can be analysed with supply availability and can commit and trigger shipments immediately. The four-day process (assuming everything goes perfectly) would be reduced to two or fewer days. That is just the start to the benefits of blockchain-enabled demand management.

Sales forecasting

Two of the major issues in sales forecasting are often referred to as "system disconnects" and "islands of analysis".

System disconnects exist when the information needed to develop sales forecasts is not electronically available to those who develop the sales forecasts. When market research information, inventory levels, confirmed orders, EDI input from suppliers and customers, and even historical demand information are not available, the forecasters simply do not have the information to do their jobs. No one can forecast accurately in the absence of accurate information. Blockchain can help cure the system disconnects by providing forecasters with electronic access to the systems that contain the information necessary to develop informed sales forecasts.

Islands of analysis exist when the users of the sales forecasts do not have electronic access to the sales forecasting system. Managers in all the functional areas of a business (marketing, sales, finance, production and logistics) need sales forecasts to do their job (every process in the business ultimately starts with a forecast of one kind or another). When these managers cannot access trustworthy sales forecasts, they might respond by manually entering data into their forecast systems. That creates extra time and opportunities for mistakes. More often, the managers get frustrated and simply create their own new and independent forecast.

These islands of analysis result in duplicated efforts. Each function forecasts without access to all the information needed, and no function has input from the other functions. And this only represents the internal disconnects. The same thing happens across companies, which means these islands of analysis are exaggerated up and down the supply chain (thus, the bullwhip effect is heightened).

Blockchain offers a potential cure for both system disconnects and islands of analysis because it provides an open, connected system, both internally and externally. Internally, blockchains used by functional areas, sales forecasting, and the other connected systems are tied together – they are all working off the same page. Anyone involved in developing the sales forecasts can access whatever information is needed – whether information is sales history, order history, market research information for regression analysis, financial plans, production schedules and/or capacity, or inventory levels. Further, this means anyone involved in using the sales forecasts can immediately provide input to the developers of the sales forecasts and conduct their own analyses based on existing sales forecasts.

Sales and operations planning

Blockchain also has the opportunity to optimize sales and operations planning (S&OP) processes, a key demand planning dimension of demand management. S&OP (sometimes referred to as integrated demand planning or aggregate planning) is fundamentally a process of coordinating demand activities (for example, marketing, promotions, pricing) and supply activities (sourcing, distribution, production) of the organization.

Executive and lower levels of management regularly meet and review projections for demand, supply, and the corresponding financial impact. Potential imbalances are identified and then a set of integrated tactical plans are created to rebalance demand and supply in a financially advantageous manner. Far too often, however, a lack of data and lack of trust in the available data are the root cause of ineffective S&OP.

A typical S&OP review meeting brings together key representatives from various functional areas from the demand side (sales, marketing), the supply side (production, logistics, sourcing) and finance. They discuss the available information in an attempt to get on the same page about the current demand and supply situations, and then they develop an integrated plan to execute based on that situation. Thus, S&OP depends on gaining the appropriate, trustworthy and secured data from customers and suppliers. When one of these is off or unavailable, the process breaks down. For instance, for a customer to share their EDI sales and inventory data with a vendor can be risky. The vendor may use these data to manage their channel inventories in ways that negatively impact the customer and help the customer's competitors.

Blockchain's permissioned capability can help overcome these issues because it can enable selectively providing and preventing access to important data. Blockchain's ability to create the combination of a public ledger with high security allows it to create a unique source of certified data that is trusted, which should facilitate better information sharing across buyers and suppliers, and thus more useful and trustworthy data used in S&OP meetings.

Demand shaping

Despite the increased accuracy of forecasts afforded by the S&OP process, forecasts often become outdated. Thus, the ability to rebalance demand and supply is crucial. Traditionally, however, the supply chain functions of the organization are tasked with responding to demand. S&OP processes in these situations result in a lopsided version of balancing supply and demand, where the supply side of the company works to current or projected demand. This is problematic. If demand exceeds supply, companies work to expedite orders from suppliers, production and shipments. If supply exceeds demand, then the company experiences excess inventory and corresponding costs. Demand shaping offers an additional, more balanced approach to matching demand and supply.

Dell Technologies is often top of mind when considering world-class demand management and provides a great example of continuously rebalancing demand with supply. If demand exceeds supply, Dell evaluates alternatives on the demand side, instead of undertaking the costly process of expediting orders, production and shipments. Dell can change product promotions and prices on its website on short notice to shift customer demand to better match available supply. When there's a shortage of components within a product, Dell removes those products from promotional lists, raises their prices and, in some cases, increases delivery times. These strategies shift demand towards other products with higher inventory.

During a US West Coast port strike a few years ago, imports from Dell's Asian suppliers were gridlocked. But Dell's relationships with its suppliers, along with its data-based strong S&OP processes, allowed them to dodge the worst effects of the strike by shifting demand and finding alternative modes of transportation to bring components in from Asia. The speed of execution of the demand shift was unparalleled. Once they became aware of the problem (the strike), the demand and supply side functions formulated a solution and shipments were being made by the following evening and continued over the next three months. Dell's swift demand shaping allowed them to grow market share during the strike, while their competitors floundered with attempts to resolve the issue on the supply side only.

You might be thinking, *Well, that is the famed Dell Supply Chain Model, and that's hard to replicate.* That's true. Dell is well known for having a unique, hard-to-copy corporate culture that enables this rapid demand rebalancing on the fly. Others see it, and perhaps understand it, but they can't do it. Building such a deeply embedded corporate culture and relationships with suppliers is indeed difficult to imitate.

Demand management that is enabled by blockchain won't overcome an awful model or a toxic culture, but it could allow companies with good models and cultures to achieve this swift, responsive demand shaping. Blockchain can almost simulate Dell's culture of rapid demand–supply reshaping because it can provide trustworthy visibility of demand and supply information across the supply chain.

Anyone who has ever tried to build consensus among a large number of players knows how challenging and time-consuming the task is to pull off effectively. But blockchain provides consensus – the information is trusted and the same information is available to all parties. There is no dispute in the chain regarding transactions because all entities in the chain have the same version of the ledger. Thus, blockchain enables parties to see problems sooner (shifts in demand or supply), and to see available alternatives (for example, substitute suppliers and different transportation routes, including financials) from which they can select to implement demand-reshaping solutions.

Consumer-connected demand management

Another seemingly unfair advantage that Dell held from the early 1990s until more recently is that it was intimately connected to its customers relative to its competitors. Its revolutionary supply chain model put it in direct contact with the market. So, for decades Dell has been able to quickly see changes in consumer demand, and thus respond to those shifts faster than competitors who are not as connected to their consumers.

Omnichannel retailing has forced companies to become more directly connected with their consumers, but many companies are still not reaping the advantages that Dell's model provides. Blockchain, however, could level the playing field for companies not directly linked to end-consumers. With consumer demand data (updated sales and corresponding availability etc) on a distributed blockchain, companies in subsequent tiers of the supply chain have the information to be agile and respond by ramping up or down production and orders quickly as consumer demand changes. Importantly, blockchain affords every player in the supply chain, not only the physical and/or digital retailer, to directly connect to the consumer, which offers substantial opportunities for improved demand management.

As we noted earlier, demand management starts with the consumer. Yet, the core functional areas in many demand management processes (for example, forecasters and operations planners) are often disconnected from those in the company who directly interact with consumers. Furthermore, consumers have historically been seen as passive recipients of supply chain management services and not directly vital or strategically important members of the chain. This view, however, is rapidly changing. The growth of mobile technology and the increasing emphasis on online retail order fulfilment have caused end-consumers to become all the more prevalent in recent years. As a result, there has been a shift towards more consumer-oriented demand management approaches. The behaviours, perceptions and attitudes of consumers are starting to serve as key strategic inputs during the design and execution of efficient and effective supply chains. A few years ago, we noted that big data was "enabling a new source of customer intimacy", and blockchain applications have now brought the consumer into the supply chain as an even more active and powerful player.

One key area where blockchain can help on the consumer side of demand management is in the area of product returns. The digitized chain of transactions that blockchain provides allows companies to accurately and quickly trace and track products up and down the supply chain. Companies could smart-tag luxury items such as designer handbags, sunglasses and shoes on a blockchain to confirm that any returned products are indeed authentic. Smart-tagging these items and loading them onto the blockchain might also impede brand impersonation, where brands of such items are copied and sold without the consumer knowing it isn't authentic.

Another area where blockchain-powered demand management can affect the consumer side is by monitoring suppliers' activities. Firms such as FieldAgent and Wegolook, through their crowdsourcing platforms, use consumers as an effective low-cost way of assessing potential and existing suppliers. Millions of shoppers become the eyes and ears for companies by checking and reporting on suppliers' activities.

The quality control of these crowdsourced shoppers has been troubling, however, with consumers finding ways to trick the system to get rewarded through payment or other means. Thus, fake crowdsourced information could inaccurately indicate that a particular supplier's product is of poor quality (poor labelling, damaged, or even out of stock). The result? A signal to the supplier to audit processes for quality control or ship more product – a little wiggle instigating the onslaught of a bullwhip effect. Blockchain, however, can verify the accuracy of the data input, and check with other data sources, to ensure the data are accurate. Then the information could quickly be shared upstream to all parties in the supply chain for effective, data-driven decision making.

What all this means to supply chain managers is that blockchain figures to help everyone involved in a product's journey gain access to accurate, relevant information that allows them to make smarter decisions when managing demand. What this means to the consumer, we would hope, is a new pair of red shoes.

Chain links: Key points from this chapter

- Blockchain can enable the real-time transfer of sales information instead of waiting for daily refresh of POS sales. In one day (or less), the transaction and inventory position data that are available on the block can be analysed with supply availability and can commit and trigger shipments immediately.

- Blockchain can help cure system disconnects by providing forecasters with electronic access to the systems that contain the information necessary to develop informed sales forecasts. Blockchain offers a potential cure for both system disconnects and islands of analysis because it provides an open, connected system, both internally and externally.

- Blockchain's ability to create the combination of a public ledger with high security allows it to create a unique source of certified data that is trusted, which should facilitate better information sharing across buyers and suppliers, and thus more useful and trustworthy data used in S&OP meetings.

- Blockchain enables parties to see problems sooner (shifts in demand or supply), and to see available alternatives (for example, substitute suppliers and different transportation routes, including financials) from which they can select to implement demand-reshaping solutions.

- The digitized chain of transactions that blockchain provides allows companies to accurately and quickly trace and track products up and down the supply chain. By smart-tagging luxury items on a blockchain, you can confirm that returns are authentic and impede brand impersonation.

- Blockchain can verify the accuracy of data and quickly share information upstream to all parties in the supply chain for effective, data-driven decision making.

References

Mentzer, J and Moon, M (2004) *Sales Forecasting Management: A demand management approach*, 2nd edn, SAGE, Thousand Oaks, CA

Supply management

09

Another capability that blockchain offers within supply chain networks is the promise of more efficient and effective procurement that's driven by extreme levels of visibility and transparency.

Blockchain doesn't offer shortcuts or redefine the basic responsibilities of procurement, but it does provide potential solutions for approaching many of its age-old performance challenges. Bringing these aspirations to life, however, will require major transitions in the procurement playbook and will come with some significant implementation challenges for buyers at every level of every organization.

Procurement, of course, is the part of the supply chain profession that makes sure organizations spend their money wisely with suppliers. It's responsible for providing a reliable supply of the various things companies need to stay in business, for making sure those needs are met in a timely manner and at the right quality level, and for ensuring that they adhere to the correct labour, environmental and ethical standards. In short, procurement is a prerequisite for keeping the factories going and the stores stocked. If procurement fails, the assembly lines grind to a halt, the factories shut down, you end up with empty shelves in the stores, and consumers go somewhere else to buy what they want.

Whether you call it procurement, purchasing, sourcing, supply management or some other term that describes spending money with its upstream suppliers, this segment of the supply chain profession has taken on a bigger and bigger role in companies over the past few decades.

In some industries, such as financial services, about 20 per cent of a company's revenue is spent on purchasing things like buildings, computer systems, facility services, IT, and the services of recruiting agencies and marketing agencies. In other industries, however, the spending is much, much higher, because it includes almost every expense outside of labour. In manufacturing, direct procurement (everything needed on the assembly line) and indirect procurement (everything you buy that supports production and sales) typically account for more than 60 per cent of revenues. It's even higher in retail, where merchandise sourcing is such a significant factor. With the rise in global outsourcing and global sourcing, these percentages have gone up in recent years and buying has become as global as the supply chain.

It wasn't always that way. In the stone ages – you know, before the 1970s – most procurement was administrative in nature. Professionals in this field spent much of their time in the back of the factory, where they mainly handled purchasing orders and invoices. This began to change in the 1980s as CFOs and corporate boards began recognizing the financial benefits of investing more resources into efforts to negotiate better, more strategic deals with suppliers.

"If I invest in a little bit of technology, invest in a team, and appoint a chief procurement officer," they reasoned, "we can drive some big savings from our suppliers. I don't have to save money – the supplier is doing it for me. It's like free money that goes to the bottom line, that goes to our R&D budget that goes to our marketing capabilities."

The commitments to technologies like enterprise resource planning (ERP) software and to giving procurement teams a more prominent place at the leadership table have led to greater and greater efficiencies and savings throughout the planning and ordering cycles. It's also opened the door for procurement leaders to focus less on administrative tasks and more on managing supplier relationships, which helps them sustain and improve negotiated deals while working more closely with suppliers on innovating best practices. The advent of more strategic sourcing not only has saved companies time and money in their regular operations, it also has set companies up to more quickly implement efficiencies after mergers and acquisitions.

Technology has been, and will continue to be, essential to procurement, because it helps create better line of sight into how much organizations are spending, what they're spending it on, who they're spending it with, and who is placing the orders. The more we can automate processes like purchase orders and invoices and the more we can use programs to analyse business needs, spending trends and other data, the more effective we can be in working with suppliers and managing those relationships.

That's why the promises of blockchain are so intriguing for procurement. With greater visibility and more automated systems, the scope of procurement's business contribution can move beyond operationally processing purchase orders, tactically negotiating discounts and strategically sourcing preferred supplier arrangements. And the engagement in supplier relationships can move far beyond assembling a supplier performance feedback spreadsheet.

Consider the following benefits that using blockchains could provide to procurement teams.

Accessing information

Using blockchains in procurement would potentially provide quicker access to accurate information used during the procurement process. For instance, many organizations still struggle to keep up with all of their contracts. These contracts differ in characteristics and rigidity, but they typically contain information on things like the price of the materials, the length of the contract, the volume to be purchased over the contract period, the penalty for defaulting, and the lead time to get the product once the final order has been placed.

Once an organization reaches a certain size and scale, it can have multiple procurement teams across different parts of the business, sometimes in several locations around the world. These teams all generate contracts with suppliers, and those contracts represent a commitment in the marketplace. But it's not easy, for example, for a team in New Jersey to be aware of a contract that's been created by a team in Mexico City, much less access it quickly. If all of an organization's spending data and overviews of all the contracts are out there on the blockchain, then, theoretically, a manager could look them up as easily as doing a Google search. That would save a lot of time and money.

Automating basic transactions

Blockchains could use smart contracts to pre-qualify suppliers, auto-generate orders, payments and invoices, and run automated reverse auctions that reduce human involvement and speed up the ordering process.

Procurement processes

The procurement process puts the "supply" in the supply chain. These are the critical cogs that keep the machine moving. The interlinked processes of strategic sourcing, the ordering cycle and supplier relations (Figure 9.1) all stand to see benefits from the promises of blockchain.

Figure 9.1   The procurement process

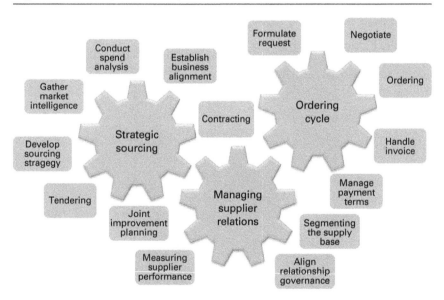

The ordering cycle is largely operational and is already highly auto-mated, but it's worth testing the benefits blockchain brings with smart contracts and with other transactional processes. In areas where multiple stakeholders would benefit from visibility, blockchain is particularly promising. But if blockchain proves itself to be just a different platform – not a better platform – then there's little reason to change.

Because strategic sourcing involves a great deal of analysis and planning, collecting data on a shared, immutable platform like block-chain could provide opportunities to leverage visibility into decision making and accelerate the process and contracting.

The visibility can also help managers more quickly spot and solve inefficiencies, which could lead to opportunities for continuous improvement discussions that fall into the realm of managing supplier relationships. These, however, represent more complex challenges, and the best initial blockchain pilots need to be simple and have straightforward goals. Testing blockchain with supplier relationships on the line is something worth trying, but only when they build on earlier, successful pilots.

Sourcing strategies

The sourcing strategies for procurement fall into two categories – those that focus on price and those that focus on value. The strategies that focus on price increase your buying power. This is the comfort zone for many procurement professionals. Those that focus on value create a competitive advantage, but these areas require more relational capital and collaborative efforts.

The chart in Figure 9.2 describes the different aspects of sourcing strategy, and blockchain figures to impact all of them to some degree or another.

Blockchain's biggest benefits, at least in the near term, figure to involve strategies that focus on price. Blockchain can add visibility into volume concentration and could make the execution of this strategy easier. Because this strategy is heavily cost-centric and focused on straight price negotiation in a relatively short price window, however, it may not be where the largest blockchain benefits are found. There may simply not be enough time in the process to build and implement a blockchain application before the negotiations are over and the procurement team moves on to the next project. When it comes to cost analysis, however, blockchain can provide data on true costs after implementing, which can lead to more accurate data for modelling and better insights for renegotiations. It also might provide better automated processes by using smart contracts for

Figure 9.2 Sourcing strategies

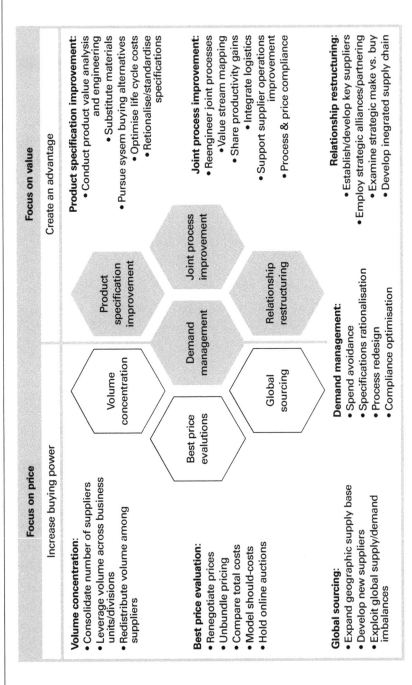

Focus on price

Increase buying power

Volume concentration:
- Consolidate number of suppliers
- Leverage volume across business units/divisions
- Redistribute volume among suppliers

Best price evaluation:
- Renegotiate prices
- Unbundle pricing
- Compare total costs
- Model should-costs
- Hold online auctions

Global sourcing:
- Expand geographic supply base
- Develop new suppliers
- Exploit global supply/demand imbalances

Focus on value

Create an advantage

Product specification improvement:
- Conduct product value analysis and engineering
- Substitute materials
- Pursue sysem buying alternatives
- Optimise life cycle costs
- Retionalise/standardise specifications

Joint process improvement:
- Reengineer joint processes
- Value stream mapping
- Share productivity gains
- Integrate logistics
- Support supplier operations improvement
- Process & price compliance

Relationship restructuring:
- Establish/develop key suppliers
- Employ strategic alliances/partnering
- Examine strategic make vs. buy
- Develop inegrated supply chain

Demand management:
- Spend avoidance
- Specifications rationalisation
- Process redesign
- Compliance optimisation

Volume concentration

Product specification improvement

Joint process improvement

Demand management

Best price evalutions

Global sourcing

Relationship restructuring

online auctions. Blockchain also promises help with transaction tracking and visibility when implementing global sourcing.

Strategies that focus on value may benefit from blockchain in the long term, but they typically aren't the best place to start with this technology. For instance, relationship restructuring can benefit from greater visibility and transparency in real time. And blockchain can uncover opportunities to improve product specifications and make joint process improvements. But initial pilots with blockchain should have safer, simpler goals. If the initial experience is good for everyone involved, then you can move on to more challenging opportunities.

Demand management is less frequently used and is a somewhat specific strategy that focuses more on how money is being spent by managing supplier demand and less on the price and supplier arrangements. A good example is the establishment of a travel policy to manage spending away from business-class and five-star hotels, instead of negotiating the price of every single hotel night. Blockchain can assist in the follow-through on this strategy by creating more real-time demand and consumption visibility and help track policy compliance without discussions with users.

Supplier segmentation

Another area of a procurement manager's toolkit that could see benefits from blockchain involves the way the manager segments the products he or she buys and the suppliers who provide them. Arguably the most common tool for supplier segmentation comes from Peter Kraljic, a former director of the Dusseldorf office of McKinsey & Company. In a 1983 article for *Harvard Business Review*, Kraljic classified vendors using two key variables: profit impact and supply risk. The profit impact represents the relative strategic importance to purchasing, while the supply risk represents the relative complexity of the market. These two dimensions formed the basis for Kraljic's portfolio purchasing model – a two-by-two matrix that further classifies products as routine, bottleneck, leverage and strategic. It's so well known that's typically referred to as the Kraljic Matrix (Figure 9.3).

Figure 9.3   Supplier segmentation

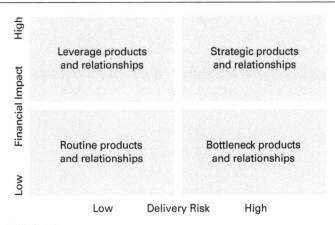

SOURCE Kraljic (1983)

The routine segment involves low-risk, low-reward items that usually don't cost much per unit and are available from a variety of suppliers. Paper clips are a common example. The value of investing in this segment is so low that there's not much reason to test blockchain here, although it might be possible to leverage the benefits from some other use-case pilots to reduce workload by automating additional processes.

The bottleneck segment involves items that have a lower financial impact, but represent a high risk to the entire supply chain. The bumper on a car might represent a small portion of the overall cost, but the vehicle is incomplete without it. Blockchain makes sense for the bottleneck segment because it can drive visibility and earlier warning about potential supply disruptions.

Items in the leverage segment represent a large share of a product's overall cost, so small changes in their price have a big effect on price and profitability. But they can be obtained from a variety of suppliers, so switching costs are low. Here, blockchain offers the opportunity to accelerate negotiations. It's a valid area for developing use cases that are cost-centric.

In the upper right quadrant are the strategic items – those you can only obtain from a few sources but that are highly critical to your needs. Healthy partnerships are essential in this segment, so any blockchain test in this area needs to be sensitive to the relationships involved. Any blockchain use case needs to be an opportunity for mutually beneficial joint innovation projects with a high level of willingness to share the risks and the rewards. A test-case failure that disrupts the relationship isn't worth the risk.

Improving risk resilience

Because so much of the risk to a company resides outside of its own walls, procurement teams are constantly evaluating how to protect their organizations from the unexpected or uncontrollable – a tsunami that hits Japan, a war that shuts down the Suez Canal, a labour strike that closes operations at a major port, or a hurricane that destroys a season's worth of crops across the Caribbean.

Blockchain can't stop a war, a labour dispute or a natural disaster, but it can help procurement teams better identify and monitor risks, while providing much-needed data to help reduce or mitigate those risks. A buyer for a carmaker, for instance, would have better visibility into what's happening not only with her supplier but with her supplier's suppliers. She then might realize that the light bulbs that go in the bumpers for one of their models are all coming from the same factory in a country where political tensions are extremely high. This would cause her to work with the supplier to ensure it has other plants that can supply the bulbs if needed. If not, she might split her contract among multiple suppliers.

Monitoring sustainability efforts

With greater insights into its supply network, procurement teams can hold suppliers accountable for ethically sourced products and more quickly end relationships with suppliers who violate agreed-upon standards.

Levelling the buyer–supplier playing fields

Transparency in the supply chain process figures to become the great equalizer during negotiations. For instance, if you want a five-year contract to buy laptop computers from my company and ask for the

"5,000 laptop discount", I could look at your purchase history on the blockchain and determine how likely it is that you will actually end up buying at least 5,000 during that time frame. So, at a tactical level, some of the old playbook might need to change, because buyers aren't going to get suppliers in a room and keep them from knowing what's happening. With blockchain, the suppliers could see what's happened and what's happening.

Deepening buyer–supplier relationships

Most successful organizations have a pretty strong mastery of the first two areas of procurement – strategic sourcing and the ordering cycle – but many still struggle with having the time and the right information to make the most of their roles in managing supplier relations. There's still not much high-quality technology, for instance, to help buyers efficiently create and manage supplier scorecards. With more information and better access to it on blockchains, procurement teams will be able to better analyse what works and what doesn't work with suppliers, then collaborate with them on improvements.

All of this promise, of course, will take time to mature. The biggest hurdle is in building private blockchain networks that strike the right balance of visibility and security. On the one hand, total visibility will become a deal-breaker for suppliers if their competitors can access proprietary information about things like pricing and sourcing. On the other hand, if only a few siloed individuals have access to information on the blockchain, it's functionally no different from current solutions such as EDI.

And, again, there are no shortcuts to the key aspects of procurement, so even a fully functioning blockchain won't be, by itself, a magic wand that solves all of a buyer's problems. A procurement officer's first obligation, for instance, is to understand the needs of the business. If he or she isn't doing that, blockchain is irrelevant. And you can't get to supplier relationships management if you don't have the ordering cycle and sourcing sorted out. Without a good functioning process for sourcing and the ordering cycle, then blockchain is only creating visibility into chaos. It's not correcting the chaos.

Blockchain only helps buyers if it complements existing processes and if there is buy-in to use it, both internally and with partners through the supply network. So, once again, we're reminded that blockchain is a maturing technology that will require time to reach a tipping point that provides its full benefits.

Chain links: Key points from this chapter

- Technology helps create better line of sight into how much organizations are spending, what they're spending it on, who they're spending it with, and who is placing the orders.

- With greater visibility and more automated systems, the scope of procurement's business contribution can move beyond operationally processing purchase orders, tactically negotiating discounts and strategically sourcing preferred supplier arrangements.

- If all of an organization's spending data and overviews of all the contracts are on the blockchain, then managers could look them up as easily as doing a Google search.

- Blockchain can use smart contracts to pre-qualify suppliers, auto-generate orders payments and invoices, and run automated reverse auctions, thus reducing human involvement and speeding up the ordering process.

- Strategic sourcing involves a great deal of analysis and planning, so collecting data on a shared, immutable platform like blockchain could provide opportunities to leverage visibility into decision making and accelerate the process and contracting.

- The visibility can also help managers more quickly spot and solve inefficiencies, which could lead to opportunities for continuous improvement discussions that fall into the realm of managing supplier relationships.

- Blockchain can provide data on true costs after implementing, which can lead to more accurate data for modelling and better insights for renegotiations.

- Blockchain can help procurement teams better identify and monitor risks, while providing much-needed data to help reduce or mitigate those risks.

- With greater insights into its supply network, procurement teams can hold suppliers accountable for ethically sourced products and more quickly end relationships with suppliers who violate agreed-upon standards.

- With more information and better access to it on blockchains, procurement teams will be able to better analyse what works and what doesn't work with suppliers, then collaborate with them on improvements.

Transportation management 10

Transportation accounts for roughly two-thirds of the costs in US logistics, or roughly $894.7 billion each year. In China, the world's second-largest economy, transportation costs as a percentage of GDP are about 8.1 per cent of total logistics costs, or 6 trillion RMB (SCMRC/DRCSPB, 2017). So, until we develop a "beam me up, Scotty" solution for moving materials and goods, transportation remains the foundation of supply chains. Indeed, transportation is the backbone of any economy and the core fundamental connector of any supply chain. If it messes up, the entire supply chain crumbles. Yet, consider the challenges companies face in managing today's transportation:

- There is $140 billion tied up every day in disputes over payments in the transportation industry (Commendatore, 2017). For an average invoice, a company waits 42 days before receiving payment. Many businesses have millions of dollars tied up in their accounts receivable.

- Processing and administration costs have risen to as high as 20% of transportation's overall costs due to over-reliance on paper transactions (Solomon, 2018). Thomas Emil Jensen, while working for Maersk Shipping and researching his PhD, said in 2015 that the physical cost of moving a shipping container is "less than half" the cost of handling the information related to it (Churchill, 2015).

- Temperature deviations are experienced by 8.5% of sensitive pharmaceutical shipments (Hampstead, 2018). These products never make it past customs because they have exceeded acceptable temperature ranges. This is a significant issue because almost 75% of common pharmaceutical products require temperature-controlled transportation, and a deviation of just 2 degrees Celsius can spoil the product. It is estimated that temperature deviations cost companies an average of $150,000 per small package shipment (iContainers, 2017).

- Ninety per cent of trucking companies have six trucks or fewer (Salama, 2018). This causes the industry to struggle with matching shippers (the demand) with carriers (the supply), which leads to a variety of inefficiencies. For instance, it's estimated that truckers drive 29 billion miles per year with partial or empty truckloads.

These challenges and others have plagued the transportation industry for decades, which is why blockchain's promise for addressing them has so many supply chain leaders excited. Here are a few of the potential solutions specific to transportation.

Blockchain promises to address challenges in these areas related to transportation:

- Freight tracking
- Carrier onboarding
- Load board
- Payments and pricing
- Fraud and theft protection
- Electronic logging devices
- Optimization of capacity, routing and scheduling
- Performance history and vehicle maintenance.

Freight tracking

Companies have been tracking freight for decades through the use of GPS technology, but GPS alone doesn't fully provide the needed information. Historically, trucking companies have used phone calls and fax machines for location updates. Then came EDI, and today we largely use APIs, the software intermediaries that allow two applications to talk to each other. These technologies, however, have run into challenges when trying to scale to meet today's fast dynamic pace. That's where blockchain comes in, because it potentially can bring the much-needed scale for real-time updates.

Blockchain also provides the benefits of trusted location updates. As information is passed through the supply chain, there are numerous opportunities for screw-ups – misinterpretations, alterations, tampering and so on – without the shipper's or owner's knowledge. Such inaccurate information results in a bullwhip of global supply chain challenges. Blockchain can simplify this process in a trusted, integrated and shared manner, because its decentralized nature prevents anyone from altering or tampering with such data.

Carrier onboarding

Any transportation manager knows that onboarding carriers can be an arduous task. It includes validating the carriers' driver records to make sure they have a strong safety rating, verifying insurance coverage and assessing whether drivers meet service level requirements.

Shippers and brokers historically have requested that carriers provide this information, which is usually shared via paper or some electronic means. Even when a broker needs extra capacity and finds new carriers available, they must go through this onboarding process of the new carriers before assigning loads. This may not sound like a big deal until you remember that there are 500,000 trucking companies in the United States (US Special Delivery, 2017). This is why many brokers and shippers have large teams of people assigned to validate carriers and manage the information for the onboarding process. And other shippers and brokers are doing the same thing because this data isn't shared.

Blockchain might address this challenge because it could validate the necessary onboarding information, store this information and make it available to everyone (Laneaxis, 2018). Shippers, brokers and carriers all could be incentivized for providing the information into the blockchain because the shared information would create efficiencies across the board. The rising tide would lift all boats... and trucks and trains and anything else carrying cargo.

Load boards

Similarly, blockchain could significantly increase the trust in, and thus the usefulness of, load board data, which have been around for more than 40 years. A load board is an on-demand freight exchange used by shippers, freight brokers, motor carriers and other logistics companies to find freight and trucks. The various shippers and brokers using load boards, however, work independently, which results in massive amounts of duplication of data and skews the forecast of needed loads. Load boards, therefore, are rarely trusted.

Blockchain would timestamp when a shipper requests a load. When the first broker posts the load, it would be visible to any other broker who subsequently attempts to input the load. Blockchain would first assess whether the load already existed by comparing the timestamped data with the original load. If a broker tried to post the same load, the blockchain would recognize the duplication and notify the second broker. There would be only one record per load instead of multiple boards, significantly reducing the outdated and inaccurate load boards that are common today. Carriers and brokers would be working off updated load data.

This also improves forecasting accuracy and enables load balancing with multiple carriers. And it could significantly reduce the due diligence steps involved in carrier compliance, because each carrier's compliance and quality service levels could be visible to everyone.

Payments and pricing

The secure blockchain database makes payment processing and settlement information easily accessible. This will allow open access to historic payment records to determine rates. Invoicing could be automated because of the shared access to multiple parties' databases. With the use of smart contracts, invoices could be triggered once a vehicle enters a geofence near a customer, followed by proof of delivery and, finally, as the vehicle exits the geofence. While RFID or other IoT devices would make this ideal, even without it the process is more trustworthy given the multiple verified data points. The reconciliation process is also substantially accelerated because all parties are viewing the same transaction.

Detention payout resolution also has long been a troubling issue for carriers that might be handled more easily with blockchain. Detention time occurs when a driver is waiting to pick up or drop off a shipment. When drivers are sitting idle and unable to accumulate miles, carriers often charge the shipper fees to cover that lost time. For instance, after two hours of waiting, a driver would receive around $50 per hour (Boblett, 2018).

Historically, however, the bargaining power of the shippers has meant that carriers were rarely able to collect those fees. The shippers generally put the burden of proof on the smaller carriers to provide documented evidence of the detention time. Even when the carrier is able to provide evidence, the shipper might dismiss it as insufficient. The involvement of brokers complicates the process and creates more opportunities for documentation to be lost and/or delayed, lessening the probability of the carrier receiving payment for detention.

The relatively recent capacity constraints in the transportation industry has swung the pendulum of power back towards the carriers, but payouts for detention fees are still few and far between. Combined with IoT electronic logging devices, blockchain provides the ability for carriers to log a driver's location via GPS, which will help support their claim that the driver was sitting idle waiting on the shipper, and thus increase the chances of being paid the detention fees.

Fraud detection and theft protection

Blockchain transactions are highly visible to everyone on the network and cannot be altered, virtually eliminating fraud. Blockchain can also include information on ID photos and rules for delivery and pickup, thereby creating a strong theft deterrent. In collaboration with IBM, Maersk is using blockchain technology to streamline the global shipping process, including replacing traditional bills of lading and integration with customs authorities, designed to make it much more difficult for criminal gangs to intercept containers in transit.

Electronic logging devices (ELDs)

In December 2017, the US government began requiring truckers to use ELDs to track their driving time. The intent is to keep drivers compliant with regulations regarding how much time they spend behind the wheel. Because drivers are paid by the mile, the ELD mandate would naturally result in drivers making less money. Yet ELDs afford many opportunities for drivers, carriers and shippers when combined with blockchain.

Data from these IoT devices potentially could be streamed to the blockchain, allowing for real-time rerouting when combined with traffic or weather data. In many cases, mandated rest times force drivers to stop at times that are not ideal, breaking up schedules and routes that result in subsequent missed loads, for which the driver would have otherwise received payment. Blockchain, however, can enable optimized routing and scheduling so that drivers' mandated rest periods are optimized to coincide with pickup/drop-off times. Ultimately, this allows drivers to utilize their allowed driving time more efficiently – more miles on the road when they are allowed – thus being paid more.

Optimization of capacity and routing and scheduling

Transactions associated with the routing decision-making processes, which involve the selection of various carriers, would be recorded on the blockchain. Thus, carriers, brokers and shippers using blockchain would have access to an enormous amount of accurate data that could be analysed. Historical records could be analysed to make more accurate demand forecasts and glean opportunities for improving future capacity plans and routing and scheduling.

The blockchain can facilitate data and information sharing between the different parties, and thus opens the door for smarter decision making when it comes to managing capacity and routing and scheduling decisions. Because the blockchain would have such rich attribute-level data (mode, carrier, pricing, routes, etc), the static and dynamic algorithms for optimal multi-modal transportation might finally be possible. As with ELDs, the ability to stream information transparently would offer a big advantage in capacity monitoring. Since capacity can change throughout the day, blockchain allows participants to observe and work with shifting capacity demands in real time. Blockchain-enabled efficient logistics of transportation can focus on shortening transportation routes, increasing vehicle load factor and reducing empty runs by improved route planning, as well as shortening the lead time and consequently reducing inventories. This would result in creating savings in transportation costs. The data collected and made available in the blockchain could facilitate financial savings arising as a result of both better combinations of loads and higher load factors, and better selections among multiple routes and the specific advantages offered by the different transportation modes.

Performance history and vehicle maintenance

According to the TMW Systems, maintenance costs have increased 50 per cent over the past five years, with 20 per cent of those costs associated with vehicle breakdowns and unplanned service events (TMW Systems, 2017). By adding all the relevant transaction metrics into a blockchain, any participant in the blockchain can see evidence of past performance – of individuals like truckers or barge captains, of organizations and of equipment. For instance, a blockchain could include all the data related to vehicle maintenance. Rather than just one person keeping these records, any authorized user could access them.

Tom Kroswek, Group Director of Supply Chain Excellence at Ryder, explained in a blog how blockchain technology could aid truck maintenance:

> Think of something as simple as a DVCR (Driver Vehicle Condition Report) that a driver populates before and after the completion of a trip. Currently this is a very paper intensive process that should convey the condition of transportation equipment to operations, safety, and maintenance. If automated and incorporated into a blockchain, all of the inspection and maintenance information could travel with the equipment throughout its lifecycle. Verification of the inspections, maintenance performance records and recall information could all be part of this blockchain. It ultimately simplifies the asset management and utilization task. (Kroswek, 2017)

Having this type of information can increase resale value, given that it would provide an indisputable history of the truck, its parts, and service. It also could help carriers and drivers with maintenance updates, such as tracking and maintaining vehicle parts. In addition, blockchain could improve the ability to predict when components might fail. Renaldo Adler, Principal, Asset Maintenance and Fleet and Service Centers for TMW, said: "Preventing just 35 per cent of unplanned repairs can save fleets thousands of dollars in hard costs alone" (TMW Systems, 2017). Recording vehicle maintenance service data and technician data into a blockchain will allow vehicle and parts manufacturers visibility of part repair and failure data that can be analysed. Historical trend analysis can then be used to predict the failure of parts, and they can proactively replace components before they fail.

Chain links: Key points from this chapter

- Blockchain can provide trusted location updates, reducing inaccurate information from misinterpretations, alterations, tampering, and other errors that result in a bullwhip of global supply chain challenges.
- Blockchain could validate driver onboarding information, store the information and make it available to shippers, brokers and carriers.
- Blockchain could significantly improve load board data by recognizing duplications and notifying the second broker.
- Blockchain provides the ability for carriers to log a driver's location via GPS, which will help support their claim that the driver was sitting idle waiting on the shipper, and thus increase the chances of being paid the detention fees.
- Data from ELDs could be streamed to the blockchain, allowing for real-time rerouting when combined with traffic or weather data.
- Because of blockchain's potential for rich, attribute-level data (mode, carrier, pricing, routes, etc), the static and dynamic algorithms for optimal multi-modal transportation might finally be possible.
- A blockchain could include all the data related to vehicle maintenance. Rather than just one person keeping these records, any authorized user could access them.

References

Boblett, C (2018) Detention Policies Need to Change in 2018 [Blog], *DAT*, 29 January. www.dat.com/blog/post/detention-policies-need-to-change-in-2018 (archived at perma.cc/DD56-X3XK)

Churchill, J (2015) Can the Cloud Lift Global Trade? *Maersk*, 25 May. www.maersk.com/stories/can-the-cloud-lift-global-trade (archived at perma.cc/8DRE-XFRA)

Commendatore C (2017) Blockchain in Trucking: What About the Middlemen? *Fleetowner*, 20 October. www.fleetowner.com/electronic-security/blockchain-trucking-what-about-middlemen (archived at perma.cc/Y9VE-K2KX)

Hampstead, J (2018) Swiss Firm Brings Blockchain to the Biopharmaceutical Cold Chain, *Freight Waves*, 23 February. www.freightwaves.com/news/blockchain/skycellblockchaincoldchain (archived at perma.cc/E77F-QLZ2)

iContainers (2017) 6 Facts About Pharmaceutical Shipping [Blog], *iContainers*, 25 July. www.icontainers.com/us/2017/07/25/6-facts-about-pharmaceutical-shipping/ (archived at perma.cc/8MQV-92F6)

Kroswek, T (2017) Blockchain: The Future of Supply Chain Operations [Blog], *Ryderexchange*, 14 March. paperblog.com (archived at perma.cc/WJ6Q-K7RW)

Laneaxis (2018) Blockchain-Based Shipper/Carrier Direct Optimization Platform [Whitepaper], 2 June, V2.1. www.laneaxis.io/assets/whitepaper/laneaxis-whitepaper-eng.pdf (archived at perma.cc/ECC3-V7NY)

Salama, J (2018) Blockchain Will Work in Trucking – but only if These Three Things Happen, *Techcrunch*, March. techcrunch.com/2018/03/02/blockchain-will-work-in-trucking-but-only-if-these-three-things-happen/ (archived at perma.cc/PTF2-E5Y8)

SCMRC/DRCSPB (2017) 2017 China Logistics Insights Report, *University of Arkansas Supply Chain Management Research Center (SCMRC) and China Ministry of Transportation Development and Research Center State Post Bureau (DRCSPB)*, September. https://scmr.uark.edu/ (archived at perma.cc/77ME-JLCR)

Solomon, M (2018) Maersk, IBM Launch First Blockchain Joint Venture for Trade, Transportation, *DC Velocity*, 16 January. www.dcvelocity.com/articles/20160116-maersk-ibm-launch-first-blockchain-joint-venture-for-trade-transportation/ (archived at perma.cc/MH44-4SCY)

TMW Systems (2017) Trimble Transportation Introduces Predictive Maintenance Analytics to Help Fleets Reduce Repair Costs, Increase Vehicle Uptime, *Trimble*, 13 August. www.tmwsystems.com/tmw-systems-introduces-predictive-maintenance-analytics-help-fleets-reduce-repair-costs-increase (archived at perma.cc/UB47-AX96)

US Special Delivery (2017) How Many Trucking Companies in the USA? *US Special Delivery*, 23 February. www.usspecial.com/how-many-trucking-companies-in-the-usa/ (archived at perma.cc/7CVD-4PL3)

PART THREE
What's the use case for blockchain?

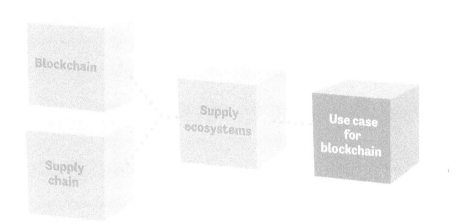

Learning from RFID   11

Philosopher George Santayana is generally credited with saying that "Those who cannot remember the past are condemned to repeat it". And over the years the word "remember" has usually been replaced with "learn from". After all, it's not enough to remember the past; if you want to build on the successes and avoid the same mistakes, you'd better learn from the past.

As we move our discussion now towards implementing blockchain, we begin with the reality that we've been here before and we'll likely be here again. So, what can we learn about implementing blockchain from previous technologies that have been introduced to supply chain management?

Since blockchain is at a stage similar to where RFID was around 2003 – lots of hype and big promises for supply chain leaders, but very little in the way of proven results from implementing the technology – we spent some time analysing the lessons learned from implementing RFID. The comparisons helped inform our thinking for frameworks you can use as you consider blockchain in your supply network.

We looked at the internal and external drivers of RFID adoption, the barriers to adoption, the path to implementation and the benefits, and then we compared those with what we've learned from early-stage case studies involving blockchain in the supply chain.

There are some key differences, of course, between RFID and blockchain. For starters, blockchain pilots appear to be driven more by executive interest and other internal drivers, whereas RFID pilots were largely pushed by external drivers such as the needs (or demands) of customers. While the use cases for blockchain may centre around creating new customer value, they are typically not driven by customer mandates or requirements. Instead, they are driven by each potential participant's internal goals – the desire to create supply chain efficiencies, to gain market share, to build consumer trust and so on.

Also, the benefits are more balanced and the cost considerations are less relevant for blockchain pilots. Unlike RFID, there are no hardware purchases and there are fewer physical infrastructure concerns with blockchain. That means there's not only no need to budget money for those concerns, but there's also no need to budget time for setting up and testing equipment.

In general, the ramp-up time for blockchain pilots can be fast and driven by narrower benefit aspirations. In fact, this is what the companies we've studied recommend – laser focus on specific goals and no scope creep. With RFID, organizations often shot for the entire laundry list of potential benefits. For now, most blockchain pilots identify a few benefits with hopes of adding others later.

What's perhaps most noteworthy from our analysis is that the RFID implementation process is very similar to what we're seeing in early test cases using blockchain, but with some important exceptions. Pedro Reyes and Patrick Jaska created a framework in 2007 that described how RFID was implemented (Table 11.1).

When we looked at how the companies we studied were moving towards implementation, we found we could overlay their approach to the RFID framework. The implementation steps for RFID don't mirror what's common for blockchain, but they are easily adopted with a few tweaks.

Table 11.2 shows what it looks like.

The differences in the way most companies went about implementing RFID and how the early adopters we studied have approached blockchain are in some ways obvious and in other ways subtler. Here are the most relevant points.

It involves more personnel

Blockchain involves an expanded network of players, both internal and throughout the supply chain. Creating a meaningful blockchain project, therefore, must involve key supply chain stakeholders and channel members. Additionally, external advisers often are helpful

Table 11.1   An RFID implementation framework

Implementation Step	Description	Personnel Involved
Step 1: Understand what RFID can and cannot do	Getting past the myths	Key personnel who will use the RFID system and IT
Step 2: Analyze current system	Analyze the processes and outcomes of the present system	Key personnel using the present system, IT, and management
Step 3: Build an ROI business case	Analysis of what potential benefits could be reached with RFID	Key personnel using the present system, IT, and senior management
Step 4: Requirement analysis	Analyze the requirements and how RFID will be implemented	Key personnel using the present system and slated to use the new RFID system, IT, and management
Step 5: Prototype testing	Test the proposed RFID system	Key personnel who will use the RFID system and IT
Step 6: Implementation	Implement the RFID system	All personnel using the RFID system and IT
Step 7: Monitor	Make sure the RFID system meets expectations	Key IT personnel and management
Step 8: Continuous improvement	Look for improvements to processes and technology	Management, IT, and key personnel using the RFID system

and, in some cases, essential for providing industry and/or block-chain expertise and experiences.

The cases we studied often started out with a few key management members, but developing the actual uses cases typically involved at least a dozen participants and usually as many as 30 in the room. In most cases, an outside expert (or team) facilitated the workshop used to identify and map the best use case.

Table 11.2 A blockchain implementation framework

Implementation Step	Description	Personnel Involved
Step 1: Understand what blockchain can and cannot do	Develop use cases for blockchain	Management and IT
Step 2: Analyze current system	Workshop with supply chain partners to map out the use case	Key personnel using the present system, IT, and management across supply chain stakeholders involved; optionally, outside consultants
Step 3: Build an ROI business case	Clear targeted benefits need to be established, but a full business case isn't necessary to pilot	Management and IT across the supply chain stakeholders and executive management; optionally, outside consultants
Step 4: Requirement analysis and pilot scoping	Analyze the requirements and how to implement the pilot; scope the pilot around achievable objectives using engaged stakeholders who can move fast	Key personnel using the current system and slated to use the new system, including customer service, operations, sales, and IT
Step 5: Pilot testing	Iterative prototyping, testing, adjusting, retesting; fast learning cycle	Key personnel using the current system and slated to use the new system, including customer service, operations, sales, and IT
Step 6: Implementation	Before scaling, a Phase 2 pilot may be necessary; also, a more detailed business case can be developed based on benefits experienced in Phase 1	Key personnel using the current system and slated to use the new system, including customer service, operations, sales, and IT
Step 7: Monitor	Few companies have reached this stage with blockchain	TBD

Table 11.2 *continued*

Implementation Step	Description	Personnel Involved
Step 8: Continuous improvement	Few companies have reached this stage with blockchain	TBD

It's more than IT

The list of key personnel using the system is broader with blockchain than with RFID. And while IT participates throughout in both, those involved with blockchain pilots stress that it is "not an IT project, but a business project". Adoption is closely tied to the involvement of key business stakeholders and to discovering real business value.

It got specific quickly

Developing an understanding of what the technology can and can't do (Step 1) was more than just a technical understanding with companies looking at blockchain. They developed and considered specific use cases for blockchain that took into account supply chain scope, which stakeholders to involve, and an initial outline of the potential pilot. It also informed which supply chain stakeholders to invite in the next steps of the process.

It requires collaborative planning

Step 2 for companies exploring blockchain typically involved a focused workshop where stakeholders came together in an offsite location to map out current and future states with blockchain. These enabled focused collaboration and a short run to the pilot.

It's not about the business case

Developing a business case (Step 3) was not a priority for the companies we studied. They came up with clear benefits and objectives to guide the project, but there was little to no effort on developing a full-blown business case. Instead, their initial goal was to test the technology in a real environment. The teams asked for support and funding for a pilot to begin to learn more about the potential of blockchain. This is possible with blockchain because the investment costs for a pilot are relatively low, especially when shared across stakeholders and when the expertise of advisers is available to accelerate and inform the process.

Its requirements provide the scope

Understanding the requirements for implementation (Step 4) became largely an issue of scoping the pilot for the blockchain projects. The key was to keep the pilot laser-focused to avoid scope creep and lengthy technology-centric development cycles. A tight, specific scope allows for fast learning opportunities. This also requires a much smaller project team than the one used to outline the use case.

It learns by testing

The companies we studied are using the pilot (Step 5) to learn more about blockchain and its real benefits. The pilot isn't a step towards implementation as much as a step towards deciding the next step. The results of the pilot could eliminate blockchain as a viable option, confirm that it's the best option, or indicate the need for additional testing (Step 6) with adjusted scope. In some cases, it might result in the need for a more detailed business plan.

It's still full of unknowns

You might have noted the big, old TBDs attached to steps 7 and 8. That's because very few companies of any size have taken blockchain to these extremes.

There's another key lesson we learned by comparing RFID's past to blockchain's present, but it's not represented in those frameworks. The lesson: competencies matter. Obviously, technical competencies are important for any business project, and especially one that involves technology. But we also found that it's important to get the best of the best, not just the most available, and that soft skills are also competencies. Some leaders felt that with the right level of executive support, motivation isn't a problem for team. But others stressed finding the right combination of realists and visionaries, with high levels of emotional intelligence.

To summarize, implementing blockchain pilots within supply networks requires management engagement and a team that's in place to plan and execute the project. An established business case isn't essential, although in some cases it can be helpful. And there is little to no need at the pilot stage for a roll-out strategy or a roadmap for a roll-out of the technology.

These are some concepts we'll discuss in more detail as we dive more deeply into what you practically need to know and do as you identify a use case and run a pilot for a blockchain project in your supply network. So, the next four chapters will detail the basic steps that can guide you on that journey – make the case, load the bus, get the party started and enter the learning loop.

Chain links: Key points from this chapter

- We can learn about implementing blockchain from previous technologies such as RFID that have been introduced to supply chain management.

- Blockchain pilots appear to be driven more by executive interest and other internal drivers, whereas RFID pilots were largely pushed by external drivers such as the needs (or demands) of customers.

- The use cases for blockchain may centre around creating new customer value, but they are typically not driven by customer mandates or requirements. Instead, they are driven by each potential participant's internal goals – the desire to create supply chain efficiencies, to gain market share, to build consumer trust and so on.

- The benefits of blockchain pilots are more balanced than with RFID, and the cost considerations are less relevant. Unlike RFID, there are no hardware purchases and there are fewer physical infrastructure concerns. There's no need to budget time for setting up and testing equipment.

- The ramp-up time for blockchain pilots generally can be fast and driven by narrower benefit aspirations so long as the participants focus on specific goals and guard against scope creep.

- Implementing blockchain pilots within supply networks requires management engagement and a team that's in place to plan and execute the project.

- An established business case isn't essential, although in some cases it can be helpful.

- There is little to no need at the pilot stage for a roll-out strategy or a roadmap for a roll-out of the technology.

Make the case 12

The decisions around experimenting with blockchains aren't easy, but they do have a common starting point. It's the same starting point leaders should use when deciding whether to embrace just about any emerging technology. Frank Yiannas put it this way: don't chase the shiny coin. "If you're chasing that shining coin," he told us, "you're doomed to failure" (Yiannas, 2017).

Blockchain, which ironically was developed to help make cryptocurrencies viable, is the shiny coin in question, and its promises for supply chain leaders can become mystically alluring. If they aren't regularly checked by reality and pursued with a noble purpose, they can turn an ordinary Sméagol into a misdirected Gollum.

"When you start looking at blockchain," Zach Steelman told us, "you can go down the rabbit hole of cryptocurrency and people get completely lost because there's so much there. A lot of it is scams – companies saying, 'We're going to magically do these things.' But it's just vapourware. There's not a lot there. It's just ideas. It's a lot of trial and error right now" (Steelman, 2018).

So, rather than falling in love with blockchain and force-fitting it into your business because of the hype, we recommend looking at the challenges you need to solve in your business and determining if blockchain – in some form or fashion – presents a potentially viable, scalable solution that's better than other alternatives.

"We're not chasing blockchain *per se*," Yiannas said of Walmart's approach. "What we're trying to do is solve business challenges. And blockchain just seems to be a technology that's going to enable us to solve some of these challenges that occur in supply chain. ... So, the advice I would have is not to be enamoured with blockchain. But if you have a business case that blockchain helps you solve, develop the business case" (Yiannas, 2017).

For Yiannas, that business case involved mangoes. And papayas. And bagged lettuce. And all the other fresh food that moves from farms around the world to the bins and shelves in Walmart's stores. The ability to more quickly trace a single bag of lettuce back to a specific farm can save money and lives when diagnosing the source of foodborne illnesses.

It's hard to overstate the effect of foodborne illnesses on the populace and the economy. One in six Americans get sick each year from contaminated foods or beverages, according the CDC's 2015 *Winnable Battles* report (CDC, 2017), and the ripple effect is staggering. An affected consumer, for instance, likely misses at least a few days of work, costing his or her employer productivity and money. Multiply that times all the people who miss work and all the associated costs, and you'll find that it adds up to some big numbers. In fact, there are more than $15 billion in medical costs associated with visits to the doctor, hospitalization and, in about 3,000 cases each year, the loss of life. Salmonella, the most common cause of foodborne illnesses, leads to $365 million annually in direct medical costs (CDC, 2017).

Foodborne illnesses

- One in six Americans get sick each year from contaminated foods or beverages.
- More than $15 billion in medical costs are associated with visits to the doctor, hospitalization and loss of life related to foodborne illnesses.
- Salmonella, the most common cause of foodborne illnesses, leads to $365 million annually in direct medical costs.
- The CDC estimates that preventing just one fatality from E Coli O157 annually would save the economy $7 million.

The US government and the companies involved spend time and money investigating each outbreak. And there's the economic impact on every organization in the supply chain – from the labourer in the field to processors to transportation providers to the cashier at the store. Again, it adds up quickly. The CDC, for instance, estimates that preventing just one fatality from E Coli O157 annually would save the economy $7 million (CDC, 2017).

And those are just the US numbers. In a global economy with complex ecosystems for supply networks, the stakes are enormous.

It's no wonder that improving traceability is such a high priority to industry leaders like Yiannas:

> The food supply today is by and large safe, but there are still problems with foodborne illnesses. Whenever there's a big food scare, what we see is that it's really hard to trace origins of food. The food system is very complex. You can't supply-chain map the food system. It's changing all the time. It's dynamic. We believe blockchain technology will enable us to do things that might result in a safer supply chain. A 1 per cent reduction in foodborne disease in the United States is equivalent to a $700 million saving to the US economy. It's profound. So, any tool that helps you reduce foodborne illness a little bit has big societal implications. (Yiannas, 2017)

Dozens of illnesses and at least five deaths in Spring 2018 were connected to romaine lettuce contaminated with E coli, according to the CDC, prompting Walmart to announce later in the year that its suppliers of spinach and lettuce would be required to participate in a blockchain programme to help improve traceability.

Yiannas says he had been chasing the "Holy Grail" of traceability for years, and blockchain provided a potential solution. Others would say the solution Walmart is using doesn't need blockchain – that it's all done with database technology that would work without being on a blockchain. But that's hardly the point. Even if it could have been done without blockchain, the reality is that it *wasn't* getting done until blockchain came along. The pursuit of blockchain as a business solution actually led to the development and implementation of a critical business solution. Whether that solution was built on the technology itself or just a result of hype-driven investments, the results have the potential to save money for the business and lives for consumers.

Yiannas "almost dismissed" blockchain as the answer in his quest because he found it complicated and hard to understand. But with some encouragement from Walmart's technology department, he stuck with it and began to discover its potential for solving the problems of his business:

The more I got into it, the more I understood the fundamentals, the more I became a believer. I encourage everyone with an interest in it or that's working on it to be multidimensional. You need to understand this. You don't have to understand how to program it or how to write the hashes or whatever. But you do need to understand the basic concepts and functionality of blockchain. Once you do that, then you'll know how it brings value to what you're doing. Let it be business-led and technology-enabled. Technology is critical, but this is solving business issues. (Yiannas, 2017)

The potential business cases of blockchain extend well beyond food safety and traceability. For instance, Bill Wilson, an industry veteran who is the global director of supply chain optimization for The Coca-Cola Company, is primarily interested in ways blockchain technology might bring efficiencies to the beverage company's direct-to-store deliveries. "I don't profess to be an expert at all," he told us during an interview in early 2018. "I have an interest in blockchain because I believe, based on what I've heard on the surface, that it will help solve some of my day-to-day operational challenges" (Wilson, 2018).

Digitizing the check-in process and the paperwork involved with their deliveries has the potential to save his company and its retail customers time and money. In Brazil, for instance, a single store delivery can take more than four hours. Even in the United States, the inventory verification process is usually hands-on and time-consuming. "There's this huge distrust that exists between the supplier and the retailer that causes us to add time to the process," Wilson said. "So, I see it as an efficiency play for us if we get that virtual handshake going."

Like leaders in countless other companies, Wilson was searching for insights on if and how to explore using the technology. Fortunately, enough other companies have now ventured down that road that others can see the most commonly used routes and perhaps steer clear of the potholes along the way.

Before the business case

Evaluating blockchain for your business begins by developing a specific use case around a specific business problem, running a pilot to test the viability and then, depending on the results of the pilot, making an actual formal business case.

The use case identifies a business problem in light of blockchain as a potential solution. It should include a budget and well-defined goals for a pilot, but it need not be driven by a fully developed business case. Instead, the questions asked and answered in creating the use case and the results of the pilot will help make (or eliminate the need for) a robust business case.

One of the most interesting insights we encountered from our research of companies that are involved with blockchain pilots, however, is that "learning about blockchain" was often viewed as a legitimate goal of the use case. Some consultants reasonably advise that you start by defining the specific business problem you are trying to solve and then ask if it can already be solved with existing technologies. If it can, then you don't need blockchain and there's no need to take the next step. That initial question certainly might eliminate some potential use cases. Some companies, however, are looking at the various promises of blockchain and then finding a business problem it potentially could solve, even if they know existing options could or already are working. The point, they say, is to test blockchain in a real environment to see if and how it works so they then can apply it to more complex challenges. IBM's Gerson said:

> I see that mainly with companies who I consider market innovation leaders. They're not necessarily technology innovation leaders. They're not necessarily number one or number two in the marketplace, but they are companies that are willing to innovate on the business model side or have a history in which failure is acceptable. … You get companies like that that are willing to innovate. They are the ones going, "Okay, everyone's trying blockchain. Now, what's blockchain all about? Let's get four or five different business groups in the room, identify five different business use cases, and let's go see what we learn."
> (Gerson, 2018)

Other companies say that they value innovation, but only pursue innovation when there's a low risk of failure.

"I've worked with clients where failure is not acceptable," Gerson told us. "They love to innovate, but if they give you money to build a minimally viable whatever, it [had] better work. That's not an innovation environment" (Gerson, 2018). The lesson, of course, is to know your culture and approach your use case accordingly.

But even the innovative cultures are chasing business value, not vapour. In every instance of that type that we encountered, there was the hope that blockchain would at least provide a better option than what already was available. And, if all went well, there was also the hope that it would be scalable. In some cases, that hope was crushed, but in others it was realized or at least remained alive after the initial testing. But the companies saw value in the learning process, even if it proved blockchain was not a viable option for the problem they were trying to solve. If all they got out of the pilot was a greater understanding of how blockchain worked (in practice, not just in theory), then they said it was worth their investment.

The point is that the return on investment can take forms that aren't smack-you-in-the-face obvious. A blockchain pilot, for instance, could arm you with knowledge specific to your company and your supply network that will be useful for future blockchain use. In this sense, it creates a readiness to take advantage of a very profitable opportunity when it presents itself.

Blockchain also could become an important business intelligence tool for obtaining knowledge about the corners of your supply network about which you know little. It could act as a catalyst of visibility, standardization and transparency between you and those corners, and, therefore, help the transition of your entire supply network to higher transparency and efficiency. Your distant partners, for instance, may still rely on paper-based records or they simply might not want to invest in a sophisticated shared database technology. The right blockchain pilot, however, could help bring radical changes to how you and your distant partners share and exchange information, what information they exchange and what they are willing to exchange with you. Rewriting the rules of engaging with your distant partners could dramatically affect things like efficiency and profitability.

Blockchain pilots typically don't require huge investments in infrastructure or extended time commitments that drive up the risks. So, larger players are often willing to front all or a large part of the costs because they know they need the participation of smaller players who otherwise might not participate for financial reasons or because their culture is risk intolerant. All of this contributes to a fertile ground for blockchain experimentation.

The use case will look different depending on the makeup and goals of each organization, but here are some basic criteria to consider.

It should have the support of senior leaders

A rogue group within a company might run a successful blockchain pilot if everyone involved brings a passion and commitment to the table. But even in that case, a lack of high-level support will inevitably result in barriers that slow or derail the process. Buy-in from top executives, on the other hand, ensures the project will be properly funded and that the participants will get the time and resources they need to have the best chances for success.

Keller called the "right sponsorship" the "number one most important dimension" of a blockchain pilot, and we didn't find a single example of a pilot that didn't have high-level executive support.

Maersk CEO Søren Skou, Kansas City Southern President Patrick Ottensmeyer and Walmart CEO Doug McMillon are among the top-level executives who have openly and actively supported blockchain pilot projects.

It should be simple

An FMCG company in Europe developed a project that involved the simplest supply chain network they could find – a farmer in the United States, the logistics supplier and the factory in Europe. The idea was to find an opportunity that's streamlined and that can be developed and implemented quickly.

If blockchain won't work with a smaller, simpler network, then it's unlikely to scale. Plus, if the project is focused on a simple, well-defined objective, it's easier to battle the types of scope creep that proved costly for technologies such as RFID.

It should complement legacy systems

Blockchain may end up replacing older systems and technologies, but that's not the goal of a pilot. Rather than focusing on eliminating existing technologies, the use case should explore if and how existing technology can provide input to the blockchain pilot. Blockchain needs data, and many of the existing technologies work well when it comes to collecting and providing data. Barcodes, EDI, RFID, the IoT – all of these figure to complement a blockchain program – if, that is, they provide accurate, relevant information.

It should have clear business objectives that block-chain might solve

Even if you just want to test blockchain to see if and how it works, you'll want to do it on a project that potentially adds value to customers and, therefore, to your business. That value can take many different forms, from efficiencies that lower the price of your products or services to track-and-trace options that make your products more marketable to health- or environment-conscious consumers. Ultimately, the goal is to improve profitability and increase market share.

Maersk's initial interest in blockchain arose from research by Thomas Emil Jensen, who wanted to better understand the paperwork and processes that were slowing down cross-border trade. He found that containers of avocados and flowers from Africa had to go through nearly 30 people and organizations, public and private, before making their way into Europe. Those parties had more than two hundred different interactions, but information was never shared broadly between people or groups and the information available was often incorrect or incomplete.

"The physical infrastructure of trade is actually pretty efficient," Jensen told Maersk blogger John Churchill in 2015. "It is the information infrastructure that is a mess" (Churchill, 2015). Back then, Jensen wasn't talking about blockchain, but about a "shipping information pipeline". But Maersk eventually used flowers shipped from Kenya as its initial blockchain pilot.

At one global consumer goods company, an enterprise architect and digital manager got the blockchain ball rolling by writing a few tech "trend reports" in 2016 that led to some presentations about blockchain. After creating awareness among executives, he began meeting with leaders of different functions who expressed an interest in doing a pilot. His hidden agenda: to get some funding so the company could start experimenting with blockchain. "Not proving it would work," he told us, "but just experimenting and learning" (Anonymous, 2018).

Leaders from all different functions quickly approached him with the same questions: *Can you tell me more? How can we start a pilot?* "The technology is looking for a problem," he told us, "rather than the other way around" (Anonymous, 2018).

By June 2018, the company had five pilots at various stages of development – three that involved supply chain management, one in finance and one involving insurance – and there was a waiting list for others. A one-on-one meeting with a procurement officer led to a use case that led to the first pilot. The two leaders quickly saw blockchain as a potential way of capturing and sharing data about the energy used by farmers to produce a particular crop used in their signature products, which made it a nice fit with their internal sustainability initiatives.

"How cool would it be if we could compare our agri suppliers on footprint?" they said. So, they created a use case around measuring the energy used to produce that particular ingredient. Later, they realized the same use case could potentially track and trace all the crops used in their products. If something went wrong with a product, it took five people 48 hours to track the origin of the problem so that they would know what to pull from which stores. Blockchain offered the potential to do it in seconds. Once they aligned on a use case, they sold it to their bosses, got a budget (about \$60,000, in this case) and started forming a team.

The objective of another pilot for this company was to reduce the number of printed documents that needed to be signed to get a shipment through a port. With the current system, getting signatures on more than two hundred documents is time-consuming, which keeps their product in port when they obviously prefer it in stores, restaurants and pubs. So, they joined a pilot with Maersk and IBM.

The most common supply chain business objectives we've seen centre around traceability, sustainability, track-and-trace, the need for trusted collaboration between supply partners, and creating greater operational efficiencies. Some business objectives have multiple impacts. For instance, using less energy to produce, store and ship a product not only saves a company money but adds marketing value among consumers who care about the environment.

"We usually end up sitting in a room with a whiteboard," Gerson told us. "We'll put up the process today, whatever it is, and then ask, 'Where's the pain in the process? What is it that you're not able to do?' Then out of that, we make a determination: is it really an immutable ledger that's needed? Because if it's not an immutable ledger, it's not a blockchain problem. There are other ways of solving the problem."

It should create shared value

Because blockchain can't succeed in isolation, it needs to provide identifiable benefits for each partner who contributes data and insights. We know of several use cases that were dropped because they only provided value to one or two key players in the ecosystem. By collaborating on a use case with your supply chain partners, you'll understand their pain points and it will help create a solution that's mutually beneficial.

There may be times when the benefit is building "good will" with another partner, but the stronger the incentive to reap business benefits, the stronger the blockchain.

That shared value, by the way, might come entirely within the construct of an internal supply chain system. For instance, a company that does business on a global scale often needs a team of people to reconcile internal financial disputes. A business unit in China, for instance, might pay the bill for an ocean carrier, but the invoice might not align with a contract signed by another business unit in England. Smart contracts would automate payments and create fewer disputes. "Then the only disputes that need to have people involved are the ones that the smart contracts don't fit," Gerson told us (Gerson, 2018).

And a shared ledger would allow everyone to see the same information, which would mean less confusion. "Today, those reconciliations are done with a lot of paper and occasionally some business process automation," Gerson said. "Since no one sees the same paperwork, people are talking on phones. Once you make all the paperwork available and it's in the blockchain, suddenly things get resolved faster.'

It should consider key markets

Kansas City Southern realized that one of its most important needs was a project that involved cross-border interactions. Primarily, they wanted to evaluate how blockchain might help more efficiently move freight from a port in Mexico, then on their intermodal trains to destinations both in Mexico and in the United States.

The use case emerged in part by asking questions about ways to expand their market share by moving more freight through Mexico. They knew the port in Mexico had fewer weather-related risks than ports in Texas and fewer labour-related risks than unionized ports in the western United States.

The problem: freight moves slowly through Mexico because it's weighed down by bureaucratic and geopolitical challenges. So, one of their key questions sounded something like this: "How do we improve the velocity and visibility of intermodal container movements through Mexico?" But the customs agencies, especially in Mexico, weren't yet in a position to partner on the project. Since the market consideration was critical, they found consultants with customs experience to replicate those roles. This allowed the project to move forward quickly, while also creating potential proof that would make the customs agencies more receptive to future projects.

It should have the potential to scale to other partners and/or markets

Every blockchain expert you encounter will likely tell you that the more partners involved and the more markets that are covered, the greater the potential power of using blockchain in a supply network. So, while you want to start small and simple, you want a project with the potential to expand. If it only works when four partners are involved, then it won't create much value.

The Maersk pilot with flowers led to new pilots with other partners who would benefit from greater efficiencies in cross-border transportation, including customers with products to ship and shipping partners such as Kansas City Southern. And Kansas City Southern is hopeful that if blockchain solves some challenges it faces with its intermodal business, those solutions might be applicable to other parts of its business, most of which would require other partners and customers in the supply network to participate.

It should strive for alignment

Ultimately, any blockchain initiative needs to align with the needs and strategies of the business. So, if you are a blockchain advocate, you need to consider the interest and support of various stakeholders who stand to benefit from a blockchain use case. You can't do blockchain in isolation; you have to work together with others in the business, or even the best use case is destined to flounder in the waves of indifference or sink in the storms of defiance.

As you consider your potential use case, consider where it falls on the chart shown in Figure 12.1. We've already mentioned the importance of executive support. So, first, how high or low is the interest from the top executives? This forms the horizontal axis. Next, how high are your ambitions for blockchain? This forms the vertical axis. This creates four quadrants, and you can plot the interest level of the business within each quadrant.

In the lower left quadrant are blockchain projects that you and the C-suite leaders have little interest in pursuing. If the rest of the business also has no interest, then the no-brainer decision is to walk away from such use-case ideas. If others in the business are asking for this type of use case, spend some time discussing the ROI and learning more with an open mind. But you need to develop genuine interesting beyond this quadrant before pursuing the idea.

If you have high interest but the executive support is missing, then you don't want to make it a priority. If others in the business see no value, then you put yourself and your team at risk if you pursue what might be a pet project. On the other hand, if you have support from

Figure 12.1 Aligning around blockchain use cases

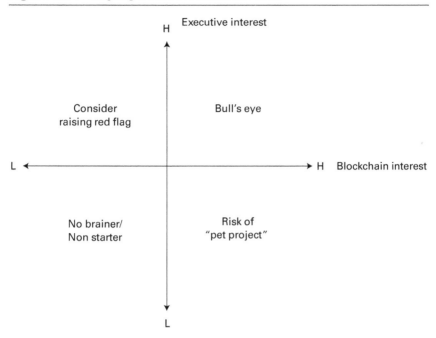

others in the business, they can help sing the praises and eventually you might wade into the test-case waters.

What if your executive team has high interest in a use case and you don't? This is obviously an uncomfortable spot, especially if there's little support from others in the business. Your role is to support and produce excellence, but to respectfully raise red flags. Don't be a jerk, but make the risks known. If others in the business also support the use case, allow them to lead and you can play a supporting role.

The bull's eye, of course, is the top right quadrant, where you and the executive team are in agreement on the value of pursuing a particular blockchain use case. If there's resistance from the business, you'll want to work hard to share the potential benefits. Implementation and adoption seldom go smoothly when they are forced. Ideally, the other business units will see the value, too, and that's where the magic can happen with a use case that has the support of every stakeholder involved.

Chain links: Key points from this chapter

- Rather than falling in love with blockchain and force-fitting it into your business because of the hype, look at the challenges you need to solve in your business and determine if blockchain presents a viable, scalable solution that's better than other alternatives.

- Evaluating blockchain for your business begins by developing a specific use case around a specific business problem, running a pilot to test the viability and then, depending on the results of the pilot, making an actual business case.

- The use case identifies a business problem in light of blockchain as a potential solution. It should include a budget and well-defined goals for a pilot, but it need not be driven by a fully developed business case. Instead, the questions asked and answered in creating the use case and the results of the pilot will help make (or eliminate the need for) a robust business case.

- The return on investment from a use-case pilot can take forms that aren't smack-you-in-the-face obvious. For instance:

  o A blockchain pilot could arm you with knowledge specific to your company and your supply network that will be useful for future blockchain use.

  o A blockchain pilot could help bring radical changes to how you and your distant partners share and exchange information, what information they exchange and what they are willing to exchange with you. Rewriting the rules of engaging with your distant partners could dramatically affect things like efficiency and profitability.

- The use case will look different depending on the makeup and goals of each organization, but here are some basic criteria to consider:

  o It should have the support of senior leaders.

  o It should be simple.

  o It should complement legacy systems.

  o It should have clear business objectives that blockchain might solve.

  o It should create shared value.

  o It should consider key markets.

- o It should have the potential to scale to other partners and markets.
- o It should strive for alignment with the needs and strategies of the business.

References

Anonymous (2018) Interview with the authors for this book, 8 June 2018

CDC (2017) CDC Winnable Battles Final Report, *Centers for Disease Control and Prevention*, 14 December. www.cdc.gov/winnablebattles/report/foodsafety.html (archived at perma.cc/G6LC-UUSS)

Churchill, J (2015) Can the Cloud Lift Global Trade?, *Maersk*, 25 May. www.maersk.com/stories/can-the-cloud-lift-global-trade (archived at perma.cc/8DRE-XFRA)

Gerson, D (2018) Interview with the authors for this book, 6 August

Steelman, Z (2018) Interview with the authors for this book, 2 February

Wilson, B (2018) Interview with the authors for this book, 10 January

Yiannas, F (2017) Interview with the authors for this book, 22 December

Load up the bus

When it comes to picking the greatest teams of all time, the choices are plentiful and the debates are never-ending.

The current NFL dynasty that is the New England Patriots just keeps rolling, but old-timers might prefer some version of the Dallas Cowboys, San Francisco 49ers, Pittsburgh Steelers or Green Bay Packers. If you're a basketball fan, you might argue for Michael Jordon's Chicago Bulls, Larry Bird's Boston Celtics or Magic Johnson's Los Angeles Lakers. The New York Yankees give baseball fans several options. You can go old school with the Babe Ruth era or more modern with Derek Jeter. You prefer hockey? How about the 1955–60 Montreal Canadiens? Soccer (*real football* outside the United States)? The Ajax teams of the late 1960s and early 1970s were a force, as were several versions of Real Madrid. Or you could go with Spain's powerhouse teams from 2007 to 2012. Rugby, you say? Hard to beat the 1986–90 New Zealand All Blacks, mate.

There's a lesser-known team, however, that might top them all. It consisted primarily of Les Clark, Ollie Johnston, Frank Thomas, Wolfgang Reitherman, John Lounsbery, Eric Larson, Ward Kimball, Milt Kahl and Marc Davis – nine men you won't find in any sports Hall of Fame. These were the animators who turned characters like Mickey Mouse, Snow White and Cinderella into icons and helped Walt Disney launch what would become a multifaceted entertainment empire.

Creating the right team is critical for any significant project, whether it's in sports or business. As Jim Collins famously put it, you need the right people on the bus. And the same is true when it comes to testing blockchain in your supply chain.

When we surveyed supply chain professionals, we found the degree to which companies had a team in place for a blockchain solution was the lowest-scoring item on average, clearly indicating there's work to be done for the engaged executives and managers who recognize the potential of blockchain.

For a blockchain use case, we found you'll likely need team members from at least three broad areas: **internal players, supply chain partners** and **technology consultants**. Additional strategic consultants might prove useful in some cases, as might leaders from established industry consortiums that have been involved in establishing standards and educating their members about blockchain.

Internal players

The internal players should be chosen based on functional contributions. For instance, if the data you plan to use will come from internal systems, then you will need someone from IT who understands the internal systems. But you will also need someone from IT who understands the data and how it relates to the project. At this point, however, you don't need someone who can actually program the platform, since that won't happen until the implementation stage.

Representatives from IT and a project manager are a must for your team, but most use-case pilots will also need leaders from other parts of the business – business operations, procurement, logistics, customer operations, customer service and marketing. In other words, don't limit the team to one or two functions. The supply chain representatives will likely come from those groups, depending on how your organization is structured. Additionally, you need to consider what types of people you need on the team.

Special projects like this sometimes end up with the *most available* people rather than the people who are *most qualified*. Those who are readily available, however, are often available for a reason – they're not already in high demand. Weak links not only don't contribute, but they also cause problems – directly if they have bad attitudes or make mistakes that must be fixed, or indirectly if you end up wasting time with efforts to work around them.

Of course, you want the best and the brightest. You want team members who are change agents, not change resisters, and who think creatively about problem-solving. The non-IT members still need to be tech savvy, and the IT members need to have basic business acumen. While it's good to have blockchain and technology enthusiasts, you also need some sceptics. Not cynics, mind you. Sceptics. You need a few realists in the room, but these realists, like the enthusiasts, need to rate high in emotional intelligence. They need to know when to push and when to pull back, which requires strong communication skills and a sense of self- and others-awareness that guides their words and their actions. We spoke with one team, for instance, that realized quickly that their blockchain pilot very well might eliminate the need for brokers in their process. When and how to address that issue, however, required sensitivity given that one of the partners on the project was a brokerage firm.

Ultimately, a team that respects each other and is aligned on the same goals will work best. While you need to avoid cynics and change resisters of the world, you need to seek out advocates. Executive support will help reduce resistance, but in the best case the project will be led by one or more enthusiasts who keep everyone not only involved but energized. "It really helped that beyond the support of the CIO and the CPO we also had an engaged procurement manager that was very willing to be on the team," one IT manager told us.

Business or supply chain partners

Blockchain has a richer use case if it involves multiple companies and stakeholders, and working with the right partners is essential to success. The use case will help define the needs, but there are several things you should consider with regard to the outside partners before moving forward.

For instance, look for partners both upstream and downstream of the supply chain, as well as partners who operate in the markets that serve the interest of your use case. That might mean that you need some partners who are nearby or others who are halfway around the globe. And you need partners who already align with you as closely as possible (or can align quickly) on standards and processes. Kansas City Southern, for instance, already captured data with certain partners using EDI. They realized that data could go into the block-chain with minimal effort on either company's part, which contrib-uted to the speed and simplicity of the project.

Perhaps the biggest decision when selecting partners for a pilot revolves around your relationship with current partners and the depth of trust in those relationships. Many of the executives we visited who have run pilots emphasized the value of keeping the pro-ject simple and working with partners you already know and trust. Yes, blockchain helps create shared trust where it's lacking, because you can trust the platform. But in the development stage, when key decisions are made and code is eventually written, you can typically move faster and smarter if there's already a high degree of respect and trust. You also want partners who are not only interested in blockchain but willing to commit to the pilot. It will cost them time, energy and, in most cases, money. You want partners who are inter-ested in the benefits and willing to invest in the discovery process. These types of partners are most often found among those you already know well and trust.

On the other hand, blockchain might offer less value when you limit the pilot to your most trusted existing partners, because you likely already have an EDI or similar link that delivers many of the benefits of blockchain. If you already have good data interchange and a significant degree of visibility with a partner, then blockchain, as we've warned previously, runs the risk of becoming a solution looking for a problem.

In fact, your most profitable partners might not want to test block-chain. For instance, we looked at Figure 13.1 earlier when we were discussing how network theory applies to blockchain and supply networks. Node B (your direct supplier) might look like an ideal can-didate for partnering with you on a blockchain pilot. If it is one of your major suppliers, however, there's probably already an effective data interchange channel in place. In this case, blockchain would be a redundant solution and you might not see its true potential. Thus, you might want to partner with one of the more distant suppliers (eg Node C). The ability of blockchain to cheaply and effectively connect you with indirect partners may bring more significant benefits.

When two or more technologies meet the minimum specifications for the functionality, customers begin to look for other deciding

Figure 13.1   Spanning a structural hole

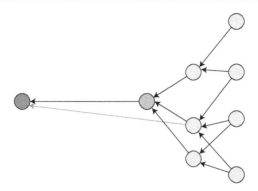

factors. Clayton Christensen's theory of disruptive innovation shows that the progression usually goes from functionality to reliability to convenience to price. Blockchain typically will not win in reliability (because of scalability, interoperability and data storage issues) or convenience (it seems complicated), so your main partners might prefer a more sophisticated EDI than blockchain.

Where blockchain really adds value is by connecting players who aren't involved in a point-to-point and who are less connected to you and each other in the existing supply chain. These pockets in your supply network are prime areas for the relative advantages of block-chain – immutability of records, transparency through total visibility for all authorized users, near-real-time updates, many users can enter data, data structured in blocks that correspond to transactions). It is within these pockets of your supply network that blockchain can start picking up its critical mass of adoption.

These partners might be less eager to test anything related to visibility and they can add to the complexity of a pilot, but there are huge upsides to working with them because they can often provide data and insights you can get no other way. For blockchain to provide its full value, you need the partners who matter most in their part of the supply network, and you probably aren't directly connected to them already.

Christensen points out that disruptive technologies and products start in traditionally overlooked corners of the world. They usually pick up a critical mass of adoption in these corners because they are cheaper or easier (but not better than the mainstream offerings). Then they disrupt (replace) the mainstream product because a lot of people already use them. Since many companies are interested in blockchain because the hype around it makes it look "disruptive", they can test how disruptive blockchain really is in one of those dark corners. For example, both of Walmart's initial pilots included using blockchain to probe such dark corners (mangoes from Mexico and pork from China).

Blockchain is cheaper and easier to install/uninstall and play with than EDI/mainstream databases, so it may truly shine (and create disruption) where visibility or interactions are very limited, such as between distant, non-trusted, secondary or tertiary partners.

A pilot only with close, trusted partners represents a toe-in-the-water approach, and some companies might need that before diving into deeper waters. At the very least, however, those deeper waters should come in Phase II as you expand and look to reap the greater benefits that blockchain offers. This is where emerging research on applying network theory can help identify the right players who are currently weak connections in your supply network.

A weak connection is one that involves relatively less communication and time together. In human relationships, it may be a distant friend – when you meet, you may have a great time but you don't meet often. In a supply chain, it may be a link you don't have much knowledge about because you don't exchange much data or information. In general, it is key partners who are in some way different. They might be in a different industry or a different country, for instance. For the Kansas City Southern Railway, the border was the main obstacle because partners on the other side speak another language and adhere to a different set of laws. Alternatively, it may be relatively new partners with whom you haven't yet established effective data and information exchange.

Just because the connection is weak, however, doesn't mean the partner is the best fit for a blockchain pilot. The partner also must be in some ways important to your supply chain as a whole. For instance, it might be the only link to a large cluster of other manufacturers about whom you have very little knowledge. There is no way for a retailer to have a thorough knowledge about every chicken producer in China. By connecting with a few large chicken manufacturers or distributors through blockchain, however, it can obtain enough information about the provenance of the most of the chicken meat flowing into its stores.

Knowing your network

Our research suggests that building a blockchain-based data interchange with a handful of companies in your supply network who play key roles may greatly enhance your knowledge of, and the effectiveness of, the deeper parts of the network. But those deeper parts are the least-known areas of most supply networks.

Managers often use their personal networks when they need to meet an impossible deadline or get information related to an important strategic decision. Often, it is through these indirect connections that crucial information is found and work gets done. For most companies, however, the indirect partners such as deeper-tier suppliers constitute the "dark universe" – they are unobservable and ungovernable. As a result, many companies tend to work with direct partners only. When a problem arises at a deeper-tier partner, managers often fall back on intuition to guide them in solving it. Blockchain makes it possible to know and develop the deeper parts of your supply network in an effective, systematic way.

Figuring out who's who in your supply network requires opening up the network and taking a deep look inside. Attempting to map the entire network at once is usually an overkill, but mapping the key players is essential. Most large companies communicate mainly with their direct, Tier-1 partners and lack any knowledge about the deeper tiers of their supply networks. So, start by identifying the functions or activities where connectivity is most needed and then think about the corresponding network segments.

McDonald's, for example, outsources its entire supply chain. It depends on a few key partners to ensure the timely delivery of everything that goes into the food it serves in thousands of restaurants around the world. These key partners are McDonald's eyes and ears in the wider world of its supply chain. They work with thousands of other suppliers at different levels. McDonald's, of course, is dependent on these key partners. If a customer complains about a bad meal, that complaint is against McDonald's and not against a farmer who used a distributor to ship a batch of bad lettuce or tomatoes to McDonald's key supply chain partner. In this case, everything that went into that meal has to be traced back to the farm of origin to prevent other food poisonings.

Companies such as McDonald's would want to identify and map the players they trust the most to keep the quality of their food at the required levels, including the farmers and the distributors who operate refrigerated facilities. They also would want to identify players they would turn to for advice for improving the safety of the food in their supply chain.

Mapping the networks, in other words, can and should be tailored to specific needs. But we have identified three types of indirect suppliers you should choose for your blockchain pilot project.

The first are **central connectors**. They interlink most other suppliers in your entire network. They are the first suppliers you notice when you look at a network map – the most connected nodes. They usually collect a lot of information from many other suppliers connected to them, so they may cause bottlenecks. Your network map cannot tell you whether a central connector is creating a bottleneck, but establishing a blockchain-based data exchange with such a firm is sure to bring you a lot of new knowledge.

Second, there are **boundary spanners** who connect different clusters of your supply network together. Without them, the network would splinter into unconnected segments. Boundary spanners are rare in any network, because most companies stay within the confines of their own cluster of suppliers. You can reap substantial benefits by identifying and engaging a boundary spanner into a blockchain-based data exchange project. The spanners usually have unique data from many segments of the network and, therefore, may become important information brokers. Thus, by engaging a boundary spanner you can leverage information flows from many parts of the network more easily and effectively.

The crucial difference between central connectors and boundary spanners is in their connectivity with the rest of the network. Central connectors have a high total number of connections (known in network theory as a "high degree centrality"). So, a company with a high degree centrality has a high number of suppliers. It may be a large company sourcing components from multiple suppliers or a manufacturer of a complex product, each component of which comes from a different supplier. In general, they are connected to a large part of the supply network that is currently invisible to you.

Boundary spanners, on the other hand, have a "high betweenness centrality". This means that their direct or indirect partners have a high number of connections. A firm with a high betweenness centrality may not have many direct connections, but its partners may be companies with a large number of suppliers. Alternatively, it may be positioned such that its direct partners also have a low degree centrality but are connected to large suppliers with a high number of partners. In any case, a company with a high betweenness centrality is located "in between" many other companies in the network. So, think about who "on the other side" can be interconnected, directly or indirectly, with the most other companies there.

Third, there are **peripheral specialists**. Usually they are manufacturers of a unique and very important component. They are located far away from the core of your network, operating on its outer fringes. Large or small, every network has outsiders. Some of these outsiders, however, may be crucial for your company's operations. They may be impossible or very hard to replace if something goes wrong.

Consultants

The third key group to consider for a blockchain pilot is the consultants who provide expertise that you can't find within your company or from your partners. For most projects, this involves a technology consultant, which could be a startup company or a larger player like IBM or Accenture. The technology for blockchain isn't complicated or difficult to create (for IT experts, that is), but other factors are important.

Here are five key questions we recommend answering as you work through the selection process:

- Are they nimble enough to meet your needs?
- How fast can they join the process and bring it to life?
- What experience do they have in supply chain? In your industry? In blockchain projects? With your partners?
- How well are they positioned to scale if the use case shows the need?
- Are they neutral in the marketplace?

Keep in mind that the right technology consultants for one use case might be different for another. If the use case needs a nimble partner that can adapt quickly to changing environments, then a startup might be more appropriate. If it needs deep experience in a global supply chain function, then a larger, more established company might make more sense.

You'll note that we didn't list public vs private blockchains as a consideration for picking a technology consultant. While some organizations might want to use a public blockchain, we anticipate the vast majority of supply chain business use cases happening on a private blockchain using Hyperledger.

Some projects also might be well served by adding additional consulting partners. Kansas City Southern, for instance, needed consultants who could replicate the role of customs agents since the real customs agencies were not ready to participate. And in one of its pilots, an FMCG company we studied brought in a research organization because of its expertise in agricultural processes.

Regardless of whether the participants are internal, external partners or consultants, they'll need to play complementary roles and bring diverse experiences, expertise and personalities. If they have high emotional intelligence, they'll work better together even in those inevitable times when there are disagreements.

"It helped that we had some realists on the team that asked tough questions to keep us honest and not get hyped up," Mike Naatz of Kansas City Southern told us. "It is also key to form a coalition of the willing and make sure stakeholders are able to act, and act fast. We had some stakeholders who were not yet ready to move forward in the pilot and we had to place them out of scope in order to keep moving – we ended up simulating their role in the supply chain' (Naatz, 2018).

Table 13.1 helps identify the basic skills, technical or otherwise, for picking your team. Each check mark represents a degree of need for the team member to have the skill. One checkmark, for instance, represents a basic level of skill, while three represents a proficiency in that skill.

Table 13.1 Skills of a great blockchain team

	Executive Sponsors (C-Suite types)	Project Managers (Internal or external)	Internal IT	External IT (Consultants who architect the systems design)	Business Unit Leaders (Internal/external)	Business Consultants (Industry or technology related)
Functional expertise (Competence in skills related to the project)	✓	✓✓✓	✓✓✓	✓✓✓	✓✓✓	✓✓
Vision (Foresight into the possibilities for success from the project)	✓✓✓	✓✓	✓✓✓	✓✓	✓✓	✓✓
Clout/Influence (Individual can motivate and move others to action)	✓✓✓	✓✓	✓✓	✓	✓	✓✓
Business Acumen (Understanding of key business drivers and strategies)	✓✓✓	✓✓	✓✓	✓✓	✓✓✓	✓✓✓

Tech savvy (Understanding of how the technology works and how to make it work)	✓	✓	✓✓✓	✓	✓
Problem-solving (Creativity when working around road blocks and executing a plan)	✓	✓✓✓	✓✓✓	✓✓	✓✓✓
Agility (Willingness and ability to change gears quickly when needed when the project calls for it)	✓✓✓	✓✓✓	✓✓✓	✓✓	✓✓✓
Realism (Insight into practical challenges and a willingness to raise the tough questions)	✓✓✓	✓✓✓	✓✓✓	✓✓✓	✓✓✓
Emotional intelligence (Communications and relational skills)	✓✓✓	✓✓✓	✓✓✓	✓✓✓	✓✓✓
Passion (Fire that burns for one or more aspect of the project)	✓✓✓	✓✓✓	✓✓✓	✓✓	✓✓

Chain links: Key points from this chapter

- Developing a blockchain use case requires team members from at least three broad areas: internal players, supply chain partners and technology consultants.

- Strategic consultants might prove useful in some cases, as might leaders from established industry consortiums that have been involved in establishing standards and educating their members about blockchain.

- Internal players should be chosen based on functional contributions in areas such as IT, project management, business operations, procurement, logistics, customer operations, customer service and marketing. Supply chain representatives will likely come from those groups, depending on how your organization is structured.

- Things you should look for in your team should include: the best and the brightest; members who are change agents, not change resisters; members who think creatively about problem-solving; non-IT members who are tech savvy; IT members with basic business acumen; blockchain and technology enthusiasts; blockchain and technology realists; members who rate high in emotional intelligence.

- Look for partners both upstream and downstream of the supply chain, as well as partners who operate in the markets that serve the interest of your use case.

- You want partners who are interested in blockchain but also will commit to the pilot.

- In the development stage, when key decisions are made and code is eventually written, you can typically move faster if there's already a high degree of respect and trust.

- On the other hand, if you already have good data interchange and a significant degree of visibility with a partner, then blockchain runs the risk of becoming a solution looking for a problem.

- Building a blockchain-based data interchange with a handful of companies in your supply network who play key roles may greatly enhance your knowledge of, and the effectiveness of, the deeper parts of the network. But those deeper parts are the least-known areas of most supply networks.

- Consultants can provide expertise that you can't find within your company or from your partners. For most projects, this involves a technology consultant that is nimble enough to meet your needs, can work at your desired speed when bringing the process to life, has supply chain and industry-specific experience, can help you scale if needed, and is neutral in the marketplace.

Reference

Naatz, M (2018) Interview with the authors for this book, 1 June 2018

Get the party started   14

Once you have a use case and you've identified the right partners, the next step is to get the party started by using whatever planning process your company or the consultant you've hired prefers.

Again, keep it simple. Create a project plan for the first three weeks that gets everyone in the room for a planning session. This typically takes about two days and it's most effective when it's held away from your office so that there are fewer distractions. The purpose of the session is, in one word, alignment.

First, align on the root cause of the problem that needs to be solved. Then align on the simplest, most straightforward solution – or what's often called a minimal viable product. Then align on the path to execute – something you can realistically pull off in eight to ten weeks. Align on the scope of the project. On the expectations for the project. On expectations of each other. On terminology. On roles. On risks. On processes… On anything and everything that might factor into the success of the project.

Areas for alignment

- The root cause of the problem
- The simplest, most straightforward solution
- The path to execute
- The scope of the project
- The expectations for the project
- Expectations of each other
- Terminology
- Roles

- Risks
- Processes
- Anything and everything else that might factor into the success of the project

It might be surprising, for instance, to discover the differences in terminology between different partners. Even in a common language environment, different organizations use different jargon, but it's particularly challenging when the project has an international flavour. The workshop provides an environment where partners can stop and ask: "What do you mean by that?" The workshop allows all of the partners to share their goals and the benefits they hope to achieve by contributing to the project.

The bulk of the workshop involves game-planning a process flow using blockchain as a solution. That, of course, begins by reviewing the current process flows and each partner's part in that process. This includes identifying current technologies each partner uses (EDI, RFID, IoT and so on) and the standards they have in place.

This is where the realists in the room often emerge with concerns about the practical implementation issues of putting data on the blockchain. So, this is where you might identify ways to work around certain barriers, or it might be where you make significant changes in the objectives for the use case.

With that in mind, you can begin creating the future state process flows using blockchain. You can define who will put what information on the blockchain, sign off on the known risks each partner is accepting, define the roles and responsibilities for planning and execution, and agree on the timing of the project, how project updates will be communicated and what will happen once the pilot runs its course.

In most cases we encountered, the sponsoring company and the technology consultant both assigned a project manager to the project, and those two project managers were responsible for the details of pushing the pilot through to execution.

Key considerations and questions

The design workshop will need some structure, which, of course, any competent consultant should provide. But here are some key questions and considerations for the design process:

- What is your current process and what pain points are causing you to consider blockchain?
- What are the pain points of your partners in this part of your supply chain?
- How would a blockchain-enabled solution compare to the status quo?
- How would a blockchain-enabled solution compare to other options?
- Reality check:
  - Where are you on the blockchain learning curve?
  - Do you have enough supply chain commitment and capabilities in place?
  - Does the solution clearly link with your supply chain strategy?
- What technical considerations must you consider?
- Answer the four W's:
  - **Why** – Why should you do this project?
  - **What** – What does success (a win) look like?
    - What is the scope of the use case? Define clear boundaries, processes and value stream map, current and future state.
    - What is the schedule?
    - What is the budget? (Vendor consultancy/implementation fees; external consultancy fees, if applicable; temporary staff to cover production inefficiencies during implementation; customization and development work; implementation team overtime during entirety of project; general staff overtime during go-live)
    - What does "done" look like? (Tangibles – things you can visibly see – that must be completed for each iteration of the agile approach to testing)
  - **Who** – Who should be involved? (See Chapter 13 on loading up the bus)
  - **Woops** – What could go wrong with the test? (A list of risks)

That last category, the list of risks that come with testing blockchain, can include any number of factors, but one of the most common in the early stages of the technology has been the unsettled issues around government regulations. If you're in an industry with cross-border operations, for instance, this is bound to come up. Regulators are also learning the ropes (or chains). Some authorities, like the port of Rotterdam and US customs, have been quick to participate in pilots and proactive about solving problems, while others have been hesitant. A key to a strong pilot design, therefore, is only to include authorities that are ready and to allow time in the post-pilot phase to work through questions from the authorities.

Stay out of the weeds

One of the most important outcomes from the workshop is to emerge with a clear statement of work that defines the scope, timing, goals and roles for moving forward. This will help keep the team focused on the business at hand, and not the shiny coin.

For the creative minds who will likely end up on this project, there's a constant pull of additional potential solutions that block-chain might offer. *If we did this*, some team members will say, *then we maybe we could solve this other problem.* IBM's Jeffrey Keller said:

> There's a desire among some to really get into the weeds of engineering a solution. I think part of the success of anything in this stage is to appropriately coach a team to stay focused on the prize of top-line revenue growth without getting overly concerned with the details that you could very quickly get into. Every step along the way, any good architect will want to look at every possible scenario, because over time there is a continual opportunity to improve a solution. Balancing that desire with the reality of budget constraints and clarity on the most important business issue you are trying to solve is another foundational element of keeping a project focused on the right components and activities.

The temptation to over-engineer the solution inevitably drives up costs. Crawl before you walk. But remember: there will likely be a

Phase II when you can walk or even run. So, keep a backlog list of ideas that you can park on the shelf until a more appropriate time.

Then what?

The original team from the workshop – which might include as many as 30 people – will remain involved, but not in every stage of the implementation moving forward. Instead, they'll stay in the communications loop except when their specific skills and expertise are required.

The technology consultant, usually in collaboration with sponsoring company's IT lead, typically writes the code. Getting the project up and running is part technology-driven and part project management – the part where someone needs to keep others on task and troubleshoot the unexpected challenges.

You'll want daily updates between some team members and weekly updates with others. You also might bring new people onto the team if you need their skills to build the platform or to do spot tests on the user experience.

What many leaders have found surprising is that this stage moves relatively quickly compared to other pilots involving a technology. Once you have the right partners and you're aligned on the process for how the pilot will work, the pilot should be up and running in as little as eight weeks.

Chain links: Key points from this chapter

- When developing a use-case pilot, create a project plan for the first three weeks that gets everyone offsite for a two-day planning session.

- Use the workshop session to align on the root cause of the problem that needs to be solved; the simplest, most straightforward solution; a path to execute that you can realistically pull off in eight to ten weeks; the scope of the project; the expectations for the project and for each partner; and terminology, roles, risks and processes.

- Allow all of the partners to share their goals and the benefits they hope to achieve by contributing to the project.

- Review the current process flows and each partner's part in that process (including current technologies and standards).

- Create future state process flows using blockchain by defining things like who will put what information on the blockchain, signing off on the known risks each partner is accepting, defining the roles and responsibilities for planning and execution, and agreeing on the timing of the project, how project updates will be communicated and what will happen once the pilot runs its course.

- Emerge with a clear statement of work that defines the scope, timing, goals and roles for moving forward. This will help keep the team focused on the business at hand and avoid scope creep.

- The original team from the workshop should remain involved, but not in every stage of the implementation moving forward. Instead, they should stay in the communications loop except when their skills and expertise are required.

Enter the learning loop

15

Innovation almost never happens in one lightning-strike moment. In most cases, it's an iterative process where an idea begets a test that produces insights that leads to changes in the original idea over and over until eventually something truly transformative emerges.

Take, for instance, the compass. The Chinese began using lodestone to create a *sinan*, or "south governor", somewhere between 300 and 200 BC. They discovered that if they freely suspended this naturally magnetized iron ore, it always pointed towards the magnetic poles. This initially proved useful for two purposes: one, for fortune-telling. And, two, for making decisions about where to do things like build houses or grow crops in keeping with the culture's geomantic principles of *feng shui*.

It was several hundred years before the Chinese began using the invention for navigation. Eventually, the compass made its way to Europe. By the 14th century, most ship captains were checking a compass rather than the stars as they navigated their way across the world's oceans. But it took time and additional experiments to fully learn the value of the compass.

Whenever a business introduces a new technology or process, there's always a learning loop that helps refine the innovation. Blockchain in the supply chain figures to be no different. In fact, because so much of the testing with blockchain in business use cases has been done in real-world businesses rather than in a laboratory, the major advancements are almost sure to come from lessons learned in piloted uses cases by business partners.

As the pilot runs its course, you are left with four basic options to consider:

- Kill it.
- Change it.
- Implement it.
- Scale it.

A pilot can last as little as a few months, but the evaluation begins as soon as the test begins. In many cases, in fact, the learning from the implementation process is as significant or more significant than the analysis that might come at the end. The initial pilot for Kansas City Southern, for instance, was suspended when they determined they needed more supply chain partners to participate if they were going to create an accurate picture of how the platform would work.

Kill it

When the pilot proves that blockchain isn't needed, the appropriate course is to learn from it and move on to other projects. For example, in the case of a global consumer products company we studied, it quickly became evident during the pilots that two of their supply chain use cases would not result in scalable opportunities to use blockchain.

One involved measuring the environmental impact of farmers who supply ingredients for their products. The hope was that it would help identify those farmers who are the most energy efficient and potentially help other farmers improve, while also giving customers visibility into the company's commitment to sustainability. But even though they chose the simplest use case in their supply network – one farmer who provided one type of crop to one factory – they quickly realized it was too complex to provide meaningful results. The ingredients from one farmer are blended with those from other farmers for consistency, so no final product would have ingredients that came from just one farmer.

Likewise, calculating the energy used for a particular batch of ingredients proved challenging. Most of their farmers grow multiple crops. So, their energy use – water, electricity, diesel and so on – must be spread over all of their crops. Doing that for one farmer was doable (and it didn't really need blockchain), but doing it at scale wasn't practical.

The other pilot that didn't seem scalable involved working with aluminium suppliers to put a scannable bar on each product that showed how much recycled materials went into it. While this worked with blockchain, it provided no clear advantages over existing methods for capturing and sharing that information.

In both cases, however, the company gained practical insights about blockchain that will help with other uses cases. "Before we move to the next pilot," they told us, "we should take a moment to evaluate the pilot. Can it be scaled or not? We do these pilots to learn from them. So, what do we take away from the pilot that we can incorporate in the next pilot?"

Change it

Thomas Edison kept failing with that whole light-bulb thing, but each failure got him a step closer to success with his bright idea. He kept tweaking, learning from what worked and what didn't. The blockchain pilots that don't fully deliver the expected or sought-after results for the supply chain still might show enough promise to call for a second attempt.

The pilot might prove that additional partners are needed, that more or different data are required, or that changes are needed in the coding or governance of the platform. Or, the results might prove that the timing isn't quite right, either because the needed partners aren't ready to participate or because there are regulatory hurdles to overcome.

Implement it

If the pilot showed that blockchain solved the business problem in a unique way that can't be done equally well with existing systems, then now is the time to implement it more fully and to look for other legitimate use cases to pilot. This is also the time to consider eliminating legacy systems that are less effective and efficient when it comes to accomplishing the same or similar goals, provided those systems aren't needed to complement the blockchain solution.

Based upon the benchmark study that we discussed in Chapter 1, we were able to analyse drivers and enablers of blockchain pilots in the supply chain – which factors do and which factors do not enable a start with blockchain? Interestingly, we found that management engagement and having a team in place are strong enablers of a successful start with blockchain. The good news is that we found high levels of executive and operational management engagement and interest in blockchain in our survey. Unfortunately, as we mentioned earlier, we also found that companies often do not yet have a team in place for blockchain. Given its importance as a critical success factor, this is an area that warrants focus in the use-case and pilot design stages, which is why we devoted a previous chapter to creating the right team. So, if you reach this step, you should have that team in place.

In Figure 15.1, the plus sign (+) represents a key need for success, the minus sign (–) represents something that's not essential and the combination (+/–) is something that may or may not be needed.

Figure 15.1   A framework for implementing blockchain

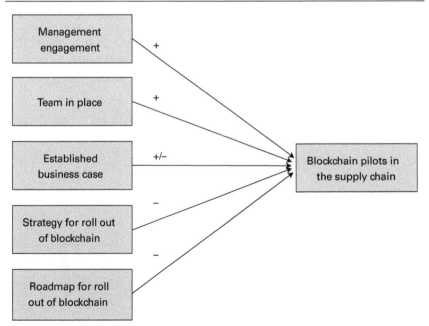

Having a business case in place matters less than having a team in place, but it still matters. A fully fledged strategy and a roadmap for blockchain implementation were not found to be significant factors in our statistical analysis. The implication of this is that in the initial stages of blockchain adoption, a bit of piloting and testing, learning and failing may be just what is needed, before a more formalized strategy and roadmap can be developed. This is good news as it reduces some internal hurdles for getting started with blockchain.

After a successful pilot, a more robust business case is worth creating to demonstrate the value to the business. This is also the time to more tightly define issues around governance. How is the lifecycle of the information handled? What information is public? What information is shared? What information is private? Does everyone agree to the same rules relative to regulation for audit? "Those kinds of questions," said IBM's Dennis Gerson, "don't tend to come up in the pilot. They tend to come up in the next phase after the pilot" (Gerson, 2018).

Scale it

The success of a blockchain use-case pilot in the supply chain will inevitably lead to additional options for using the technology. For starters, the systems architects who were forced to stay focused on the use-case goals will now be eager to dig into the backlog of ideas they created during the process.

The next question becomes, "Who else might benefit from this platform?" If one farmer and one distribution centre took part in the pilot, for instance, now might be the time to expand to every available farm and distribution centre in the supply chain. And if it worked with mangoes, maybe it's time to try it with papayas or lettuce. Walmart, for instance, went from mangoes to more than 30 food supply products by the fourth quarter of 2018.

Or maybe the use case can be expanded to new parts of the supply chain. For instance, Maersk helped develop a platform that originally focused on shipping flowers from Africa to Europe, but the success of that platform has led to use-case pilots with other products (like beverages) and other logistics companies (like railroads). Helping others address their pain points in the supply chain could lead to new or expanded business, or it might simply improve the overall efficiency of the ecosystem.

Blockchain may also offer the ability to scale processes in complex supply systems in ways where previous attempts have failed. That's the case, Yiannas told us, with the food supply. "What we're doing now," he told us, "is doing this at scale with big companies with multiple products and showing that this is scalable. ... Nobody has as much food on the blockchain as we do. It's real data on real systems. It's not hocus-pocus. It's not a pilot. It's legit. We're no longer in pilot stage."

Yiannas loves the results he's seen in food safety, but he's even more excited about how blockchain could eventually change supply chains as a whole. "People relate it to food safety, but that's just the tip of the iceberg," he said. "Some of the benefits you are hearing from me, that's all good and I'm happy about that. But I see the real value of blockchain in smarter supply chains" (Yiannas, 2017).

Maersk provides perhaps the best example of scaling blockchain. The shipping company began by working with IBM on what it called a "shipping information pipeline". This evolved to become the TradeLens platform, which goes beyond testing what works and actually attempts to build a broad platform around a realistic business plan. And *evolved* is really the key word, because almost everything about this project changed as Maersk and IBM began working with additional partners and potential partners. Indeed, even the ownership arrangement for TradeLens shifted from a joint venture to more of a collaborative model that spread the equity opportunities and governance among early adopters, emphasized the open nature of the platform and began providing solutions beyond just Maersk or even just shipping. White told us:

> The whole intent between IBM and Maersk coming together was to establish an industry platform, an open, neutral industry platform. We decided to go with this collaboration model, which enables some of those issues to be addressed in a broader way. The dialogue we've had continues to be strong, even strong with some of the participants who had some concerns. ... I've spent a number of hours (in 2018) making

sure we're aligned on how to make this happen and, most importantly, communicating with all the ecosystem participants that we've had on board'. (White, 2018)

When Maersk and IBM gave an update on TradeLens in August 2018, there were 92 participants involved in the early adopter programme and more signing up each week. "I don't know if 92 is a good number or a bad number," White told us. But more important than the number of participants, he said, was:

> the range of ecosystem participants – from ports and terminals to inland providers to customs agents. ... We've started to get ocean carriers and regional carriers involved, so the dialogue has changed quite a bit. At the time (August 2018), I think we had some 154 million events related to the shipments that were on the platform, and that's growing almost a million a day. ... I think what it speaks to is the breadth of information that's available and what I think is a high level of engagement of the industry to try to find a solution for what we're doing. (White, 2018)

TradeLens, in other words, was beginning to see some momentum as it scaled:

> What's interesting about that is you become more and more data-rich as you have more network participants, as you get more customers involved, and those customers get some of their transport partners involved, and that really helps us continue to evolve the platform. That's why we call it early adopter, because those who sign up early really help us try to shape this thing. (White, 2018)

Those early adopters are helping define the actual functions the blockchain might perform, but also the governance and the future of the platform. White said TradeLens has created an industry advisory board to review the product's road map to help ensure it meets the needs of the market and to address the ongoing issues around collaborative standards and interoperability.

White is aware that TradeLens will likely have to work with other options in the marketplace as TradeLens and those other options begin to grow. Otherwise, participants in highly open supply chains – those who work with multiple partners downstream and upstream

– could be overly burdened by the need to invest in and use multiple platforms. White said:

> We know there's a number of initiatives out there. I can only imagine what supply chain leaders are going through trying to assess and identify all these projects and initiatives. … We haven't seen anything so far that really nears the broad scope of what we're attacking with the TradeLens platform, but it's hard to see the future. None of us have a crystal ball, but it's hard to imagine that there'll be only a single solution for whatever issues or opportunities are going to be addressed. … We're growing and developing, but we're not going to develop all of the solutions ourselves. (White, 2018)

Those solutions might work with TradeLens or as new applications on the TradeLens platform.

Ultimately, White points out, there remain a great many unknowns. Scaling a blockchain project, he points out, is very much a journey that requires patience, resilience and flexibility.

"We've come a very long way in a short period of time," he said, "but you know what? There's a long way to go. There's a long way between where we are and getting the bulk of global trade from a carrier participation standpoint" (White, 2018).

With scale, of course, come new challenges. Something that was inexpensive and fast-moving during a small, well-controlled pilot might become slower and more expensive as it expands. The additional participants who are needed to make for a data-rich environment also add layers of complexity for both the functions and the governance of the platform. And the rush for results often comes at the expense of due diligence. White said:

> At the end of the day, if we're not careful we will have replicated some of the problems in our manual sort of archaic paper-based processes and have just as complex, maybe more so, digital solutions tomorrow. It's really important that we continue to focus on these things and make it as standardized and open [as possible] for companies to participate so that we can spend time enhancing the value rather than just trying to find out how do we marry information between different parties. (White, 2018)

Chain links: Key points from this chapter

- Whenever a business introduces a new technology or process, there's always a learning loop that helps refine the innovation. Blockchain in the supply chain figures to be no different.

- As a pilot runs its course, you are left with four basic options to consider: kill it, change it, implement it or scale it.

- When the pilot proves that blockchain isn't needed, the appropriate course is to learn from it and move on to other projects.

- Blockchain pilots that don't fully deliver the expected or sought-after results for the supply chain might still show enough promise to call for a second attempt.

- When blockchain solves a business problem in a unique way that can't be done equally well with existing systems, then implement it more fully and look for other legitimate use cases to pilot. This is also the time to consider eliminating legacy systems that are less effective and efficient when it comes to accomplishing the same or similar goals.

- After a successful pilot, a more robust business case is worth creating to demonstrate the value to the business. This is also the time to more tightly define issues around governance.

- The success of a blockchain use-case pilot in the supply chain will inevitably lead to additional options for using the technology, including new features or expanding to additional partners.

- Scaling a blockchain project is very much a journey that requires patience, resilience and flexibility.

References

Gerson, D (2018) Interview with the authors for this book, 6 August 2018

White, M (2018) Interview with the authors for this book, 28 August 2018

Yiannas, F (2017) Interview with the authors for this book, 22 December 2018

Off the chain 16

The future of supply chain management will include blockchain. The question now is really more of degree. Will blockchain become another in a long line of technologies that have tweaked the way products move to market? Or will it create a sea change?

As we've seen, blockchain has the potential to make supply chain processes better if for no other reason than by providing greater visibility. But more importantly, it can make entire supply chains, and their members, better at making things better. Indeed, that's ultimately the greatest potential impact that blockchain may have on supply chains – that it might generate the continuous improvement of existing and new processes, whether within inventory management, demand management, supply management, transportation management or any other aspect of the industry.

While companies have increasingly used continuous process improvement approaches across their suppliers (for example, via supplier development programmes), most are still largely focused on internal workflows. In addition, these initiatives are still largely centralized and owned by one company in the supply chain. The result, at best, is improvements to pieces of the supply chain – pieces that when improved may have little actual effect on, or could even potentially degrade, the overall supply chain. Indeed, this is classic sub-optimization of the parts instead of optimizing the whole.

The decentralized peer-to-peer aspect of blockchain, its integrated version of a single source of truth and its distributed ownership combine to enable continuous process improvement and learning to move from the company level to the supply chain level (upper right quadrant in Figure 16.1). Blockchain will allow multiple parties in the supply chain – even in complex, dynamic networks – to understand and analyse processes across all of the companies involved. The largest constraint – the limiting factor that is preventing the supply chain from achieving its goal even when nothing goes wrong (or the

"Herbie", if you've read Eliyahu Goldratt's classic bestseller *The Goal: A process of ongoing improvement*) – can be identified much more easily, enabling the key supply chain participants to collaborate on addressing that constraint, instead of wasting time on what amounts to the trivial in many areas in the supply chain.

Figure 16.1   The impact of blockchain on supply networks

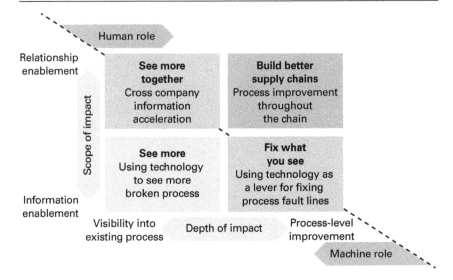

Where to begin?

Talk to any flavour of process improvement manager, whether its lean, Six Sigma, agile, or design thinkers, and they will tell you the most important first step to any process improvement is to understand the customer. The second, they'll say, is the crucial step of grasping the current situation, which most often is initiated through the use of visual process or value stream maps. The reason this is such an important step is that it gives you the global picture that makes it possible to understand the current condition of your supply chain. Understanding your current condition is the necessary precursor to both visioning a future state of your supply chain that is better and making needed improvements to reach that vision.

Mapping the supply chain, as we noted earlier, is much more challenging and complicated than mapping a manufacturing plant or distribution centre. While many organizations have conducted process mapping exercises and have process maps for internal operations, tactics and strategies, very few have been able to do so for their supply chain. Corporations often have hundreds, if not thousands, of suppliers, each of which have numerous suppliers, transportation providers and service providers.

Some companies may have a list of these first-tier suppliers, but it would be a rare exception to have a map of the connected supply network all the way back to the source of their products. Even rarer is the number of supply chain managers who have a full understanding of this complexity. Recently, organizations such as SourceMap – an MIT Media Lab research project startup – have provided the ability to visualize entire supply chains. But these are still limited largely to static supply chain maps, and are nowhere near complete.

Blockchain adopted and implemented across a supply chain, however, would provide the necessary means to possess real-time, dynamic, updated supply chain maps. As they grasp the current situation via the blockchain-enabled supply chain process maps, waste can be identified and attacked through process improvement principles, techniques and tools. Thus, when companies want to improve their supply chain processes, the blockchain-enabled supply chain maps can be accessed easily and quickly to begin the process improvement activities.

For example, as mentioned earlier, all improvement efforts start with deeply understanding the needs of the end-consumer of the supply chain and the value they need the supply chain to add for them. Blockchain's characteristics facilitate sharing of enormous amounts of consumer data across the supply chain. The data afforded by blockchain are also more objective and trusted, and thus more reliable and representational for the participants in the supply chain to collectively better understand consumers and unique consumer segments from an evidence-based perspective. With a deeper understanding of what a supply chain's specific consumer segments do and do not value, actions can be taken to eliminate the most important non-value-added activities in the supply chain. Some consumer segments, for example, may place a higher emphasis on shorter delivery times and other segments may place a higher emphasis on lower costs. With blockchain's near-real-time visibility of activities through-out the supply chain, leaders can better identify and remove delays in transportation, production and sourcing to speed up delivery or reduce cost, depending on the objective they're trying to achieve for the consumer.

Functional improvements

In addition to providing the ability to visualize the supply chain to initiate significant process improvement projects, the real-time visibility afforded by blockchain provides an additional important functionality to improving processes.

After decades and decades of process management successes and failures, researchers and experts have concluded that there are two core, insightful principles that make all the difference in managing and improving processes. Are you ready for it? Here it is:

1 Problems will occur.
2 Because problems will occur, they must be made visible immedi-ately (Spear and Bowen, 1999).

We bet you are just blown away by this earth-shattering insight! Well, it may not seem to be much of a revelation, but Toyota understood these principles and did everything they could to make their pro-cesses as visible as possible. Too often, problems occur in processes and they go unnoticed until it is too late, which wreaks havoc throughout the company and the supply chain. The visibility pro-vided by blockchain would allow real-time detection of problems.

Most organizations struggle to master their processes and, as a result, they struggle to be successful. Ironically, processes in supply chains are increasingly invisible. Supply chains once processed and tracked activities using paper, but they now use supply chain infor-mation systems and databases. And yet, we can't see the data as easily as we could with paper-based systems. Paper provided some level of tangibility – we could touch it. Now, supply chain activities increas-ingly occur in somewhat of a mysterious, invisible way. Because they are invisible, it is hard to see when things go wrong. The common question raised in meetings – "Where are we with such and such?" – is often answered with blank stares and silence. And it is hard to communicate what the process is supposed to be when it is all managed by some enigmatic server somewhere in the Cloud.

Today's supply chain complexities obviously make going back to paper a silly suggestion – there are far too many moving pieces and data. But existing supply chain systems are fraught with major gaps in missing data, inaccuracies and lack of trust.

Blockchain-enabled visibility may overcome those limitations. It provides the ability to more accurately and fully capture the current situation – again, the foundation for improving anything. And it enables processes to be managed visually in a trusted and useful manner. Managing visually allows us to easily see whether what is actually happening is meeting the standard of what should be happening. When out-of-standard conditions are made visible at a glance, people can respond quickly and easily. People must know, and be able to easily see, if what is happening is in standard (what should be happening) or is out of standard (a problem). Root cause analysis can then be conducted more rapidly, and quality can then be built in at each step.

For instance, when a defect in a part occurs early in the supply chain or when a food is contaminated, you can obviously remove the affected part or food quickly – maybe even before it reaches customers. More importantly, making that problem visible faster allows you to perform root cause analysis on why the problem occurred in the first place, and run small experiments and analyse data afforded by the blockchain to assess what happened at the supply chain level. Even better, the blockchain allows data to be shared globally across the supply chain. Rather than company-specific data alone, data can be easily captured at high intervals (perhaps every minute), assuming the blocks can be created at the necessary speed.

The availability of these data in an immutable format and in almost real time allows analyses of variances to identify when processes are heading out of control before the problem occurs. Such analyses, perhaps through Six Sigma control charts, provides information on whether variances in product specifications (eg food safety metrics) are natural variances (nothing to be concerned about) or variances that indicate that a process (eg refrigeration) is heading "out of control" and needs to be examined at a deeper level before problems occur.

What's next?

Supply chain managers who are good at continuous improvement find ways to make their processes visible. They invest resources into capturing what they do. One of the principal benefits of this is a shared understanding about processes and policies. Once things are visible on a map, you can decide where you want to go and how to improve the process. That allows you get better and better over time. Small improvements compound over time to create a real competitive advantage. Thus, blockchain can be a powerful enabler of continuous improvement. That's the sea change it can potentially create.

The future of blockchain for supply chain leaders remains a bit murky, of course, but the potential improvements, as we've demonstrated throughout these pages, are easily worth the investments. Those investments will create some headaches, they will take us down some dead-end roads and they will even put us in a few ditches. Eventually, however, they will take supply chains into a future that's better than it's ever been.

Reference

Spear, S and Bowen, H (1999) Decoding the DNA of the Toyota production system, *Harvard Business Review*, 77 (5), pp 97–106

APPENDIX
Where's your highlighter?

You no doubt read this book with pen and highlighter in hand, furiously taking notes and marking those passages that raise questions or provide answers and direction for your particular situation. When you close the covers of this book, we hope you don't set it on a shelf to collect dust. We hope you refer regularly to those notes as you think through blockchain's role in your supply chain. In fact, we believe it will come in handy as you think through the ways just about any new technology might affect your links in the supply chain.

This chapter should be a handy place to start when looking for the lessons learned. So, let's compare notes, shall we? Here's a summary of some of the key findings based on our interviews, case studies and research. Add to it as you feel necessary and use it to improve your supply chain processes.

Use-case development considerations

The findings from our case studies offer several considerations that managers can use in developing use cases for blockchain in supply chain:

- Blockchain is an enabler, not the solution itself; avoid the risk that comes with a "solution looking for a problem".
- The hype surrounding blockchain creates some positive outcomes; it can be used to drive executive interest.
- There are no shortcuts to victory; if you have poor master data, blockchain will give you better visibility into poor data.
- Internal drivers matter more than external drivers. Even though customer considerations are important, projects can be self-initiated. Unlike with RFID, a lot of pilots are not driven by customer requests or mandates.

- Focus on process and people, not on technology. Among other things, this reduces the risk of blockchain being a "solution looking for a problem" and it helps address the fact that having a team in place is a critical success factor.

> "The technology underneath blockchain is not new, nor is it the hard thing. What matters more for a use case and a feasible pilot is finding a process where blockchain holds potential and finding a team and group of stakeholders who really would like to engage." – IT manager

- When identifying processes, focus on a multi-constituent process where greater visibility can enhance supply chain effectiveness. In those settings, the potential of driving greater visibility across stakeholders holds great merit.
- When identifying partners for a use case, focus on a set of stakeholders who are willing and able to engage and where there already exists a high level of trust.
- Do not limit the stakeholder environment to internal partners from one function. Involve different functions of the supply chain (such as procurement, logistics, operations, IT, commerce, customer services), and consider both suppliers and downstream supply chain partners. Involving external experts or consultants can accelerate use-case development as well as pilot development and potentially help fund the pilot.
- Do not limit the definition of effectiveness to speed and customer service. While these are potential benefits of blockchain, other important factors include environmental visibility, reduced counterfeiting, lower administrative costs, and food safety.

Pilot design factors

These pointers will help as you manage the design of a blockchain pilot:

- Do not focus on eliminating existing technology. Instead, explore how existing technology can provide input to the blockchain pilot. Blockchain may be more about making existing technology better. Use it to accelerate the ramp into the pilot, rather than blowing up existing infrastructures and installed bases. Blockchain can benefit from many existing technologies and enhance their value and use.

- Do not aim to automate broken processes. If you do, you will end up with automated but still broken processes. Look for processes with improvement opportunity. Use blockchain to fix processes, not simply automate the status quo.

- Keep the pilot team small, the scope limited and the scale manageable.

- While consultants can certainly help sell blockchain internally and supplement a team with capacity and capability, do not become overly dependent on them. Otherwise, you may not be able to drive the internal learnings and capability development that can sustain blockchain beyond the pilot.

- The composition of the team matters, both in functional expertise and in personality types and emotional intelligence levels.

> It helped that we had some realists on the team who asked tough questions to keep us honest and not get hyped up. It is also key to form a coalition of the willing and make sure stakeholders are able to act, and act fast. We had some stakeholders who were not yet ready to move forward in the pilot, and we had to place them out of scope to keep moving – we ended up simulating their role in the supply chain.' – supply chain manager

Post-pilot considerations

Blockchain remains an infant technology, and most pilots will end with questions as well as answers. Here are several areas for further learning past the initial pilot stages:

- Stop to learn from the pilot. At one company we studied, for instance, there was a rapid rise in interest among leaders through the company who wanted to partner with IT on piloting new use cases.

> Before we move to the next pilot, we should take a moment to evaluate the pilot. Can it be scaled or not? We do these pilots to learn from them, so what do we take away from the pilot that we can incorporate in the next pilot?' – IT manager

- Automation and information benefits are frequently experienced in the pilots, but transformative benefits are rare. In terms of the blockchain implementation framework, most pilots result in "seeing more" or "seeing more together". Some also result in "fixing what we see". There are few examples of where blockchain is used to build a better supply chain. This is partially due to the intentional narrow scoping of many pilots.
- A successful pilot will raise new questions about if or how to scale.

> "Scaling from one material supplier to several may cause an explosion of data entry needs on the supplier side, that suppliers may not be ready to provide with quality and speed. It adds cost and complexity for suppliers when multiple partners further down the value chain are demanding more data through different proprietary solutions." – Cameron Geiger, Senior Vice President, Walmart

- Leadership interest and management engagement may be sufficient to get started with a blockchain pilot. And given the small investment requirement for a pilot, a full business case may not be needed. A more detailed business case, however, certainly will be needed to move from pilot to large-scale implementation.
- Technological limitations may also surface in the post-pilot stage. The need for computing power for large-scale blockchains may reach a point where it may actually slow the chain down.
- While consultants can certainly help sell blockchain internally and supplement a team with capacity and capability, do not become

overly dependent on them. Otherwise, you may not be able to drive the internal learnings and capability development that can sustain blockchain beyond the pilot.

RFID comparisons

In addition to pilot design considerations, our research reveals a few unique characteristics about blockchain pilots that may be different from RFID implementations:

- Costs for piloting blockchain are generally far less of a barrier than the cost of testing RFID. Whereas RFID requires investments in hardware, most blockchain pilots involve only a modest investment of management time and a small coding budget.
- Blockchain pilots can move quickly. The coding needed to get pilots up and running typically only takes a few weeks (six to eight). Initiating an RFID pilot often involves more time because you need to bring in hardware and set up a physical testing environment.
- The benefits and costs may be more balanced in blockchain pilots. In RFID implementations, retailers tend to experience more of the benefits and manufacturers more of the costs.

Red flags

The nine biggest barriers to blockchain adoption are: collaboration, standardization, interoperability, bureaucracies, competitive instincts, immutability, security, garbage in, and cost.

Blockchain becomes much more powerful for supply chains and adoption will come much more quickly when it is combined with technologies such as IoT, analytics, machine learning and AI.

The pilots we studied that did not move to implementation often had a combination of the following:

- Wrong partners: Key constituencies were not involved in the pilot and/or were not available to take part in a more scaled version.

Figure 17.1 A summary framework for decision making

Use case considerations

1) Internal focus, with eyes for customer value creation, but not driven by customer mandate
2) Focus on identifying right process and right team
3) Focus on multi-constituency processes
4) Focus on stakeholders willing and able to engage but do not make the team too big
5) Involve upstream and downstream supply chain parties and hire consultants for faster access to lessons learned elsewhere and for coding support
6) Consider a definition of success beyond the focus on efficiency; sustainability and revenue/customer impact potential also

Pilot design considerations

1) Do not focus on eliminating existing technology, bring it into the blockchain platform to make the platform better and leverage existing beyond its current application (eg get more out of it in stead of replacing it)
2) Don't automate broken process, use the pilot to fix it
3) Can we build a team that is not overly dependent upon consultants?
4) Keep the pilot small and targeted, use a backlog list to avoid scope creep
5) Consider team composition (ex: a realist on the team helps)
6) Build in a learning loop at the end of the pilot
7) No need for full strategy and roadmap at the pilot stage

Further learning areas about blockchain

1) Size of benefits; administrative and informational only or also transformational?
2) Ability to scale beyond pilots?
3) How to develop a business case to justify investment needed for larger-scale implementation?
4) Technical limitations? Speed of computing, inter-operability?
5) Limited focus of standard-setting underway given the nature of international supply chains

Swing thoughts throughout the pilot stage

1) Blockchain technology is an enabler of improvement, not the solution itself
2) Consider using the hype around blockchain potential to drive interest in pilots
3) But be aware that there are no short cuts to victory; in order for blockchain to work we need to stop ignoring hard to solve basic problems such as quality of master data, collaborative tensions, poor adoption of best processes
4) Where consultants help? Driving the hype to get executive interest in blockchain
5) Where this does not help? In figuring out how to move from interest to application – this is were most companies are currently in the dark

- Lack of trust: There was not a base level of trust for designing a platform that shares data, even within a trusted blockchain environment.

- Governance: The blockchain remained closed and controlled by one dominant supply chain player and it didn't work for smaller upstream supply chain partners.

- Interoperability: Multiple players who were needed for a broader implementation were working to develop different blockchain platforms. The various parties thus needed to wait and see if or how the different platforms would work together.

- Standards: Key issues on standards were still unsettled.

- Regulations: Governments and other agencies were continuing to work though oversight issues.

Figure 17.1 shows a summary framework for decision making.

INDEX